FOUR DEGREES CELSIUS

ADVANCE PRAISE FOR
FOUR DEGREES CELSIUS

This is a well-crafted story that captures the heart and the imagination. It portrays in colourful detail the hardships suffered by both the lost members of the MacAlpine Party and the group of dedicated searchers. The author has presented a picture of the sheer determination of Cruickshank and the pilots and air engineers who overcame almost insurmountable odds to safely bring home all of the missing adventurers. What could have been a tragedy was instead a triumph, and credit must be given to the Inuit who contributed generously and unselfishly wherever they were needed. If you enjoy a tale designed to keep you glued to your seat from beginning to end, this book is for you.

— Rex Terpening, author of *Bent Props and Blow Pots*

Kerry has used the diaries of her grandfather Andy Cruickshank, one of the search pilots, and Richard Pearce, one of the survivors of the MacAlpine Expedition, to bring a human dimension to the technical aspects of the 1929 aerial search and rescue as well as some new information. What is already a riveting story is all the more fascinating when Kerry brings to light that lessons learned from the survivors were applied in the NASA space program.

— Shirley Render, author of *Double Cross*

Kerry Karram

FOUR
DEGREES
CELSIUS

A Story of Arctic Peril

DUNDURN
TORONTO

Editor: Jane Gibson
Copy editor: Jennifer McKnight
Design: Courtney Horner
Cover design: Jesse Hooper
Printer: Marquis

Library and Archives Canada Cataloguing in Publication

Karram, Kerry
   Four degrees Celsius : a story of Arctic peril / Kerry Karram.

Based on Andrew Cruickshank's diary.
Includes bibliographical references and index.
Issued also in electronic formats.
ISBN 978-1-4597-0051-2

   1. Search and rescue operations--Canada, Northern--History--20th century. 2. Western Canada Airways Limited. 3. Prospecting--Canada, Northern--History--20th century. 4. Canada, Northern--History--20th century. 5. Cruickshank, Andrew David, 1898-1932. 6. Bush pilots--Canada, Northern--Biography. I. Title.

FC4161.K37 2012   971.9'502   C2011-908016-8

1   2   3   4   5   16   15   14   13   12

 Conseil des Arts   Canada Council  Canada   ONTARIO ARTS COUNCIL
du Canada   for the Arts   CONSEIL DES ARTS DE L'ONTARIO

We acknowledge the support of the **Canada Council for the Arts** and the **Ontario Arts Council** for our publishing program. We also acknowledge the financial support of the **Government of Canada** through the **Canada Book Fund** and **Livres Canada Books**, and the **Government of Ontario** through the **Ontario Book Publishing Tax Credit** and the **Ontario Media Development Corporation**.

Printed and bound in Canada.
www.dundurn.com

Front cover image:
The Fokker Super Universal G-CASQ crashes into the icy waters at Burnside River, Nunavut. *Courtesy of Western Canada Aviation Museum.*
ice © Trevor Bauer/iStockphoto
Back cover image:
Andy Cruickshank in the Arctic. *Karram Family Collection.*

Dundurn	Gazelle Book Services Limited	Dundurn
3 Church Street, Suite 500	White Cross Mills	2250 Military Road
Toronto, Ontario, Canada	High Town, Lancaster, England	Tonawanda, NY
M5E 1M2	LA1 4XS	U.S.A. 14150

To Andrew, Victoria, and Mikaela

When you listen with your ears, you begin to hear.
When you listen with your mind, you begin to think.
But when you listen with your heart, you begin to care.
— EGH

Table of Contents

| Foreword |

In the latter half of 1929 there was heightened public awareness in Canada's Far North of the disappearance of the MacAlpine party, a group of prospectors seeking to find rich mineral deposits in what was then the Northwest Territories, but is now Nunavut. They had departed Winnipeg in their fleet of aircraft on August 21 for Churchill, Manitoba, and arrived at Baker Lake on September 7. They left two days later for the Arctic coast and from this point on there was no further news of their whereabouts. It was after they were forced down that the MacAlpine party had to wait for rescue on the shore of the Arctic Ocean.

This would mark the start of one of the greatest aerial searches in Canadian history. It would test the endurance of both men and their machines in a hostile environment of summer and winter flying conditions. The accounts of the events that took place over the next three months are a tribute to members of the MacAlpine party, their "Eskimo Saviors," and the pilots and engineers involved in the search. It would rivet the attention of other nations and become one of the epochal stories of Canadian aviation history. There have been other articles written on this event, but information has recently come to light that provides new insight into this story.

Every undertaking of this nature must have a leader in the field, and the person selected to be "chief pilot of the search"[1] was Andrew Cruickshank, a pilot for Western Canada Airways. As a former First World War pilot, Royal Canadian Mounted Police officer, a founder of the first Yukon airline, and a pilot with extensive northern flying experience, Andrew was the logical choice for such an undertaking. The conditions under which the search took place created horrendous logistical challenges for both men and their machines. Because of the close proximity to the magnetic North Pole their compasses were unreliable. There were incomplete maps for ground reference and no weather stations or radio communications for assistance. Flying by "dead reckoning" in adverse weather of fog and snow was a navigational challenge that presented formidable hazards to taking off and landing on unknown surfaces.

Andrew was a man with perseverance. His flying skill carried him through situations that would challenge a qualified "instrument-rated" pilot of today. In spite of the airplanes breaking through the ice, dealing with broken undercarriages caused by landings on rock hard snowdrifts, and flying basic aircraft of the time, he motivated his engineers to make remarkable repairs with whatever was at hand. His dedication to the mission never overshadowed his patience under stress or his respect for the resourcefulness of his engineers and pilots. On occasion they were forced to wait to be rescued from their downed or damaged airplanes, often in bitter cold weather, and with insufficient supplies.

This account is the manifestation of Andrew Cruickshank's concern and compassion for humanity. He was dedicated to his profession as a pilot and exhibited extraordinary northern flying skills. It is a story of heroism, set in a region of extremes.

Kerry Karram is the granddaughter of the late Andrew Cruickshank, who was killed in 1932 on a flight from Great Bear Lake to Fort Rae in the Northwest Territories. The title of this book, and the story it tells, might better be titled *Kerry's Journey*, for it has revealed to her, and members of the Cruickshank family, previously unknown events in her grandfather's past. Kerry diligently gathered information from many sources to write this story and pay homage to one of our great northern "bush" pilots. With the advent of the airplane, these were the people who were instrumental in opening the vast Canadian North.

Believe me, you won't want to put this gripping Canadian account of survival back on the shelf until you have read the last word.

Gord Emberley CM
Lac du Bonnet, Manitoba

ACKNOWLEDGEMENTS

It began in Yellowknife, at the Float Plane Fly-In, July 2007. I was with my son, Andrew, at the dedication of a bronze plaque to my grandfather Andrew David Cruickshank, commemorating his contribution to bush flying in Canada. At this event I met Gordon Emberley, a most delightful man who is dedicated to documenting and preserving Canada's aviation history. I posed a question to him: "Can you tell me about the Dominion Explorers expedition of 1929?"

With a smile, Gord answered, "A good start would be to read the diary of Richard Pearce, but you will never be able to find a copy of it." My interest was ignited and the hunt was on. I did manage to find a copy of this incredible diary, a very rare published version, in a used bookstore in Sydney on Vancouver Island, of all places. I was enthralled and could talk of nothing else, it seemed, during that year.

My son Andrew quietly commented one day, "Mom, you need to write a book. This story deserves to be told. The spirit which Canadians are known for is encapsulated in this remarkable tale." Thank you, Gord, for sparking my interest, and thank you Andrew for putting forth the idea and for having faith in me.

Throughout this adventure I have been supported and encouraged by many others. Marti Sevier, of Simon Fraser University, was my right hand. She has read multiple drafts of the manuscript and had clear, insightful comments and questions that spurred me to do further research. She "unblocked" my writer's block and came to the rescue time and again with a calming influence. What a joy to work with such an inspiring friend.

Murray Peterson, who works through the Manitoba Archives and the City of Winnipeg's Historical Building Committee, was my archival researcher and consultant extraordinaire. Thank you for unearthing such a plethora of information and for scanning many of the images contained in this book. I am forever grateful for your involvement.

Pam McKenzie, from Western Canada Aviation Museum, thank you for your assistance with archived photos. They make the story come alive.

I am also indebted to two enthusiastic supporters: Ulrich Lanius, who has encouraged me to "say what I want to say" and who gave me the confidence to pursue this project; and to David Pol, a big hug and thank you! And to Eleni Papavasiliou who came to the rescue in sorting out the PC/Mac issues, and helping out in other areas as well. Thank you.

David Stephens and Bryan Fitzpatrick, thank you for your help and encouragement in the early stages. Gordon Emberley, Clark Seaborn, and Rex Terpening assisted in unravelling the workings of the Fokker Super Universals for me. Thank you for your explanations and input in how to explain things correctly.

Thank you to Richard Pearce's daughter Margaret Hall and to grandson Rick Hall for chatting with me about the story. How exciting to get to know Richard Pearce's relatives … wow. And to Daryl Goodwin, thank you for allowing me to view and use your grandfather's photos.

Thank you, Barry Penhale, for your encouragement and efforts on my behalf. And Jane Gibson, my editor, thank you for being everything I thought an editor would be. You both played a tremendous role in bringing *Four Degrees Celsius* to print, and ensuring the integrity of the story was kept. Also, thank you Jennifer McKnight, my copy editor, for making sure every *i* was dotted and the manuscript was polished for print.

To Ed, Julie, David, and Christopher, thank you for the "thumbs up" and for your continued support.

Mom, thank you for keeping the boxes of family memories safe and for that very special phone call October 17, letting me know you "found it!" Your father's diary was a treasure kept for decades and gave us Andy's voice to tell the story. Auntie June, thank you for the keen interest you have shown in this book and for paving the way for me.

And finally, my deepest gratitude, as always, goes to my family. My husband Michael; children Andrew, Victoria, and Mikaela; and son-in-law Steve. You give my life meaning.

INTRODUCTION

A few years ago an eighty-year-old diary surfaced from a box in a North Vancouver basement. This was pilot Andy Cruickshank's diary and log, documenting the search for the MacAlpine expedition of the Dominion Explorers during the fall of 1929. In terse, spare prose, Andy wrote, "The following is a copy of my diary while on the MacAlpine search. My idea in jotting down a few notes each day was really to enable me to reconstruct the whole story at any time. It is my intention to write such a story when I can find time to do so." Unfortunately, timing was not on his side, and he never wrote the story as he intended. I have been able to research and locate many details related to the MacAlpine expedition, and I hope that this attempt to achieve his goal would have met with his satisfaction.

Andy Cruickshank, who led the search party, was my grandfather. As a child I would listen to my grandmother Esmé

Cruickshank's tales of this adventure, all of which captivated my attention. Later, upon meeting other bush pilots, I realized that his story was one that I wanted to share.

Using Andy's diary in tandem with Richard Pearce's diary, the dramatic story unfolded. Pearce self-published his journal in 1931, in a very limited edition, for those who took part in the remarkable adventure of opening Canada's North for the development of its resources. The slim book, bound in burgundy fabric, was signed by Pearce himself, and although not handwritten, as is Andy's diary, it feels to me as if he, along with my grandfather, was giving permission for this extraordinary tale to be told.

But it was only when I began to research and learn more of the background of this search and rescue that I understood that it not only concerned a group of courageous men and women, but it also, in a very real way, reflected an important aspect of Canada's history that resonates to this day.

| MAPS |

During the years between 1845 and 1848, Sir John Franklin mapped thousands of miles of the Arctic's coastline. By the 1920s, aerial photography for mapping and surveying had been established. Andy Cruickshank, an avid photographer, took photos for Western Canada Airways out of his plane windows while flying in the north. In 1925, the Interdepartmental Committee on Air Surveys and the National Air Photo Library began an extensive archive of aerial photos, and because of this, Canada has one of the most comprehensive storehouses of aerial photographs. (*www. nrcan.gc.ca/earth-sciences/products-services/satellite-photography-imagery/aerial-photos/about-aerial-photography/942.*)

The following maps show the advances made from the use of aerial photography.

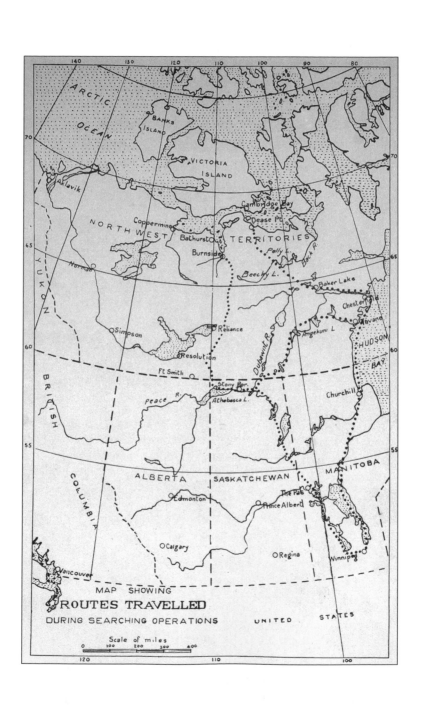

MAP SHOWING
ROUTES TRAVELLED
DURING SEARCHING OPERATIONS

Scale of miles
0   100   200   300   400

Maps of the 1920s were vague and sparse, often created by cartographers relying on second and third hand descriptions. Pilots learned to follow the rivers and lakes to help them determine their route. During winter in the North, when lakes and rivers were frozen, this method of "steering the course" was almost impossible. Radio support for navigation was non-existent and ground communication spotty. Cruickshank's search and rescue team flew along the route marked by the dotted line. What is so amazing is that their route almost matched the route flown by the Dominion Explorers. These early flights will go down in Canadian history as truly remarkable.

From Richard Pearce, Marooned in the Arctic: The Diary of the MacAlpine Aerial Expedition, *1929*.

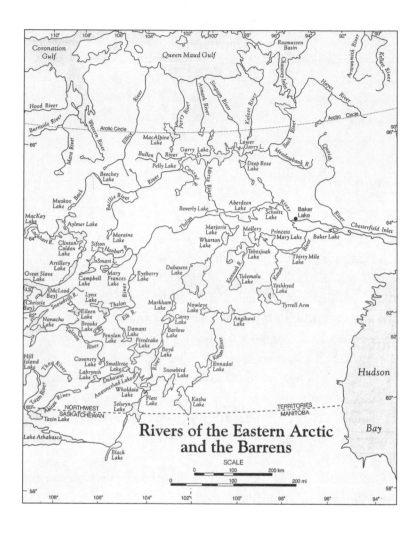

Rivers of the Eastern Arctic
and the Barrens

The current map shows, in detail, some of the rivers and lakes that likely both the MacAlpine party and Cruickshank's Search and Rescue group followed during their flights. Wholdaia Lake, at the northern Saskatchewan, Northwest Territories border, was the fuel depot transfer location. The search pilots then flew with fully loaded planes up the Wholdaia River over the chain of lakes to reach Dubawnt Lake, then westward to Baker Lake where the change over to skis was made. The flight from Baker Lake to Burnside River, roughly 400 miles (flying in a straight line) passes over a lake now named MacAlpine.

Map from Canoeing North Into the Unknown *(Toronto: Natural Heritage Books, 1997), 100.*

| ONE |

Leaving for the Barrens

September 20, 1929
Richard Pearce's Diary

This is zero hour at Stony Rapids. We were due there to-day and there is quite a lot of talk as to how our absence will be dealt with. If Bathurst wireless station is working we have no doubt planes are searching for us now....

The Dominion Explorers Expedition (Domex) left Winnipeg on August 24, 1929. Seven men aboard two planes lifted into the sky and headed northward. Their goal was ambitious: a 20,000-mile flight across northern Canada. The plan was to head north to Hudson Bay then along the west shore to Chesterfield and Baker Lake. From there, they aimed to fly westward to Pelly Lake along the Back River then follow the Western River to Bathurst. Upon reaching Bathurst, they would head southwest to Dismal Lake and along the Arctic coast to the Coppermine River, up the Dee River to Great Bear Lake, and on to Fort Norman, then head north again to Aklavik. From Aklavik they would follow the Mackenzie River to Fort Simpson, and continue on to Fort Reliance along the Slave River. Following the Slave River they would proceed to Lake Athabasca, The Pas, and then return to Winnipeg. Their mission was to pick up Domex prospectors and to do some surveying. The men would also check on the Domex bases and bring in winter supplies.

The expedition was comprised of a small group of seven men. Major G.A. "Tommy" Thompson piloted G-CASP ('SP), a Fokker Super Universal leased from Western Canada Airways (WCA). He was accompanied by his twenty-five-year-old mechanic, Don M. Goodwin; forty-three-year-old Colonel Cyril D.H. MacAlpine, president of Dominion Explorers Ltd.; and thirty-six-year-old Richard Pearce, the editor of *The Northern Miner*. Twenty-eight-

The Fokker Super Universal, built in the 1920s, was a conventional high-wing monoplane. The weight of the fifty-foot wingspan was supported by a cantilever construction. It could land on wheels, floats, or skis, making the aircraft well adapted to withstand the conditions of Canada's North.

Courtesy of Daryl Goodwin.

Richard Pearce stands beside the plane, ready for the Dominion Explorer's expedition.
The Pearce brothers purchased The Northern Miner *in 1916. This newspaper would be*
considered the voice of the Canadian mining industry.

year-old Stan MacMillan piloted Fairchild FC-2W2, CF-AAO ('AO) (owned by Domex), accompanied by his mechanic Alex Milne and E.A. "Brodie" Boadway, a Domex mining engineer and pilot. Boadway was twenty-eight and Milne was twenty-five.

From the air, the Barrens seemed to roll on forever — its vastness stretching beyond any visible boundaries. There was no place for the eye to pause or to rest. Below the stretched fabric of the fuselage, steel-coloured lakes seep from gashes in the landscape where, true to its name, nothing much grows other than surface root flowers, mosses, lichens, grasses, and an occasional twisted willow. Known in the summer as the wettest desert in the world, every depression in the land is filled with water, some of which finds a way to empty into massive, sluggish rivers. This land is both hauntingly beautiful and forebodingly harsh, and its immense size has a power that fuels the imagination.

In August, when the planes took to the sky, autumn in the North was just ending. When one is heading towards the northern latitudes, a mere three hundred miles can make the difference between one season and the next. Despite the starkness of the landscape it was a beautiful time. As one pilot observed of the northern fall, "The hills were tinted with exquisite colours obtainable only through the artistic endeavors of frost."[1] The intense brilliance of autumn flares only briefly before the onset of a cold, inhospitable, dark winter, but, for now, one would have thought that nature, decked out in its flora in golds, greens, reds, and purples, was preparing for a celebration. However, her malevolent side was soon to emerge.

Colonel MacAlpine had chosen to ignore the warning of experienced pilots who cautioned that the expedition had been scheduled too late in the year. Indeed, he felt he had no choice. A feasibility probe was crucial in order to avoid any further loss of claims for Canada's metal and mineral resources. Domex had been recently beaten by Cyril Knight Prospecting in the race to stake a claim on a nickel deposit in Rankin Inlet. When stormy weather had grounded Domex planes, Jack Wilson, working for Cyril

Knight, had ignominiously trumped the aerial prospectors by travelling in a canoe! Ironically, the same stormy weather that had immobilized the Domex planes had swept the Knight prospectors directly to shore at the claim site.

In the 1920s, aerial prospecting was in its infancy, but, despite setbacks like this, still offered the advantage of covering vast areas in a relatively short time. From the air, mining geologists and prospectors had a panoramic view of the mineral-rich rock below, where thousands of northern lakes made it possible to land almost anywhere on floats. These resource hunters sought rust stains, which indicated the possible presence of iron ore, copper, or nickel, or streaks of white, often quartz veins, which, if they were lucky, would be speckled with gold. Zinc, radium, pitchblende, oil, diamonds, emeralds, and rubies — the Canadian Barrens were a wealth of riches for the taking. The newspapers of the day characterized expeditions like MacAlpine's as "the quest for the golden fleece."[2]

Cyril MacAlpine's vision was that through the development of its natural resources, Canada would become a civilized nation. He was a gold-medal graduate of the University of Toronto in 1907, prior to completing a law degree from the University of Manitoba.[3] In 1928, MacAlpine teamed up with four of Canada's top mining men, establishing a publicly traded company called Ventures Limited. Brothers Thayer and Holstead Lindsley, Joseph Errington, and Major-General Donald Hogarth, along with MacAlpine, were developing Falconbridge Nickel Mines in the Sudbury Basin. Its stock had a value of $14.85 in August 1929.[4] MacAlpine was a strategist, setting up bases at Bathurst Inlet, Baker Lake, Stony Rapids, and Tavane with gas and provisions, which would allow airplanes to penetrate further into the Barrens. Because the Dominion government of the time took little interest in mining, it was private businessmen like the Dominion Explorers who financed and flew out in search of mineral wealth. In fact, it was the early prospectors and bush pilots who initially propelled this exploration of the North.

The Canadians were by no means alone in their quest. American investors and prospectors were hot on their heels to lay claim to the riches of the North. The stock market was on the boil, and money flowed like rivers, fuelling the frenzy to strike it rich. But Dominion Explorers had their "ace in the hole" with Thayer Lindsley.[5] In mining circles he was known as the man who could look at rock and rock formations and see the potential inside. He also had tremendous personal wealth and used this to strengthen Dominion Explorers. The transformation of the Northwest Territories from an area of hidden wealth into a mining mecca was beginning to occur with electrifying suddenness, and the aircraft was at the heart of the transition. Domex had access to planes, cash, and expertise. They were a force to be reckoned with — a group of men who met the Northern revolution head-on. This late expedition into the Arctic was meant to be complete before the end of float-flying season. Heading north into the Arctic to lay more claims at this time of year with the use of planes equipped with floats was still viable, though risky. However, the new claims would add value to the developing holding company of Ventures Limited.

As the Fairchild and Fokker headed north, they encountered haze produced by bushfires, and the rising hot air created updrafts, bouncing the planes around like toys. Flying in these conditions rattled not only the plane, but also the nerves and bones of the passengers. To the bush pilot, however, this was part of the fun, because he knew literally how to "fly by the seat of his pants." Feeling the air pressure and wind currents under his seat, he deftly worked the controls to keep his fragile craft on course.

On this expedition, Thompson and MacMillan dexterously navigated the bumps and grinds of the turbulent air to reach their destination, landing safely on floats at Churchill, 640 miles north of Winnipeg, by late afternoon on August 26. Upon arrival they anchored the Fokker 'SP and Fairchild 'AO in the harbour. There they awaited the arrival of the *Morso*, a ship that was bringing supplies to equip the expedition, the Domex bases, and northern posts for winter.

When the *Morso* failed to appear, Stan MacMillan and Colonel MacAlpine flew out in 'AO to search for it but had no luck. The mystery of the missing ship was solved, however, when two lifeboats carrying the crew of the *Morso* and its captain were sighted heading toward Churchill Harbour the following day. Captain Mack explained that fire had broken out in the engine room from a carelessly tossed cigarette[6] and the crew had narrowly escaped before the dynamite and fuel-laden ship exploded. The Domex men decided to keep both planes at anchor — 'AO at the RCAF buoy and 'SP out in the harbour — in case a crew member, who had been badly burned, needed immediate evacuation.

During the night, while the men slept, 'SP dragged its two twenty-five-pound aircraft anchors and went out on the riptide, and was drifting away.

August 28, 1929
Richard Pearce's Diary, Churchill Harbour

Awakened at four this morning by Thompson, who reported that the CASP had dragged its two anchors and drifted out to sea. The tug Graham Bell had reported passing the plane in the tide rip. At daylight the plane was spotted by the SS *Acadia* five miles out, with all but its wings submerged. The *Acadia* towed the SP for an hour when it was decided to try to lift it out of the water. The rope used in hoisting parted and our ship [plane] sank. When the Acadia pulled her anchor, the plane was found hooked to it and the wreck was hoisted onto the steamers deck. It was brought to Churchill at 6 p.m. and in the meantime Western Canada Airways was notified at Winnipeg and the reply was received that Buchanan was leaving for Churchill at once [with a replacement plane].

Courtesy of Daryl Goodwin.

Fokker Super Universal G-CASP lies in pieces after its immersion in Churchill Harbour. The wings of the plane were cut off so the wreckage could be hoisted and carried onboard the SS Acadia.

On August 28, Colonel MacAlpine wired Prime Minister Mackenzie King, requesting that Ottawa send the tug, the SS *Ocean Eagle*, and the tow schooner, *Neophyte*, to bring winter supplies and gas for the northern communities that would otherwise have been served by the *Morso*. Still optimistic, he did not yet realize that his carefully plotted expedition had already begun to come apart at the seams. To further complicate matters, on August 29, Domex's second plane, Fairchild CF-AAO, pulled its anchor and drifted out on the riptide to the mouth of the harbour. Luckily, this plane was successfully towed back to shore.

Since conventional wisdom among bush pilots maintained that flights into the Arctic should never be attempted singly, MacAlpine decided to postpone his expedition until the replacement aircraft arrived from Western Canada Airways. This was the Fokker Super Universal G-CASK, piloted by Roy Brown (not Buchanan as originally expected). But, en route, 'SK was hampered by forest fire smoke and developed carburetor trouble, so it did not arrive in Churchill until September 6. This delay put the expedition even further into the in-between season before freeze-up, when takeoff and landing would be impossible. Most planes flying into the Barrens landed on lakes, which required floats to stay afloat in the summer or skis to land on snow or ice in winter. During the in-between season a plane could not land safely. Neither of the MacAlpine expedition planes had skis, which would be needed once the lakes froze. In the autumn, even ground travel became difficult, if not impossible. The ice frequently wasn't thick enough to hold the weight of a human being, and travel by boat was risky, hampered by shifts in weather, which could whip up the water and swamp small vessels.

Such concerns were far from the pilots' minds on September 7 as they took off, aiming to reach Chesterfield, 230 miles to the northeast. After refuelling there, they decided to spend the night and they had a "good party," sharing their food, cigarettes, and chocolate bars freely with the residents — a show of generosity they would later regret. Major Robert "Bob" Baker joined the group, hitching a ride to the Domex base in Bathurst Inlet, where he would take over as manager and the expedition would restock their supplies. This brought their number to eight.

As the planes readied for takeoff on September 8, 'SK developed carburetor icing — a common and sometimes deadly problem among bush planes because of the North's high humidity, which caused high condensation in the carburetor. As a plane rose into the air, colder temperatures froze the condensation, reducing or even blocking fuel intake. The carburetor icing delayed them until 5:30 p.m. The pilots encountered snow squalls and turbulence with increasing intensity and ferocity and only succeeded in reaching Beverly Lake before the last light. It began to rain, and the men split into two groups — one spending a wet, uncomfortable night in a tent and the other a cramped, uncomfortable night in the cargo area of one of the planes.

September 9 saw more setbacks. Storms began to blow and visibility became poor. Relying on their magnetic compasses at such a high latitude posed another problem, since their position near the North Pole rendered these devices unreliable, owing to the difference between true and magnetic north. They were now in the region on maps called the "area of compass unreliability."[7] The navigators had been using sun compasses, but frequently the sun was behind storm clouds and could not be seen, making this form of navigation almost impossible as well. These navigational limitations were a serious matter, especially since the terrain below was both unfamiliar and unmapped.

This meant that the Domex pilots could not "track crawl" from Beverly Lake to Bathurst Inlet, either. Track crawling was a technique used in navigation whereby the pilot would draw a line on his chart from his departure point to the destination point. As he flew over the land, he would ensure he passed over surface features portrayed on the map.[8] However, since this area in the sub-Arctic was unmapped, this was not an option. It was, therefore, even more critical to have clear skies for sun-compass navigation. With the sun's visibility increasingly blocked by clouds, the pilots headed in a more northerly route hoping that this would guarantee their sighting of Bathurst Inlet. This navigational technique was called "dead reckoning."

They continued to fly over bleak tundra where there were no lakes and thus no place to land. The situation became tenser as they entered another cloud bank. Somehow they managed to communicate the need to land, and fortunately found a small, shallow lake. After a brief discussion, they decided the safest option would be to head to the Arctic coast and follow it to Bathurst. Thought was given to the possibility of being stranded due to weather, so the men decided they would be less likely to be frozen in if they waited it out on the ocean. Both planes took to the cloud-filled sky again and headed in the direction they thought was north and the Arctic coast.[9]

Fuel was being consumed at an alarming rate and the pilots decided there was no room for further uncertainty. They had better land. When they dropped below the clouds they could see "a big bay," which they assumed was Bathurst Inlet. Much to their delight, they spotted an Inuit camp and lined up for landing. Early bush pilots and explorers knew the importance of finding such settlements when experiencing difficulty. Because of the Inuit skill in surviving the ruthless conditions of the Arctic and their unquestioning willingness to share whatever they had, from food to clothing and knowledge, they were an invaluable lifeline. The pilots landed on the choppy water, cut the engines, and floated towards the shore. It was all hands at work as they pulled the planes ashore. Immediately, they were greeted by a Cogmollock Inuit family.

The Cogmollock Inuit population lived in the wilds of northern Canada around the Dease Point, Kent Peninsula, and Herschel Island areas where snow and ice covered the ground for most of the year. They were used to blizzards that raged for weeks at a time and the temperatures often below -45°C. Conditions were tough and unforgiving and bitter winds screamed down from the North Pole, yet this group was skilled at predicting weather and thrived on the far reaches of the Arctic Circle. The Cogmollocks were also successful hunters of seal, white fox, and polar bear, and used these skins as trading commodities.[10]

One of the first people they met, and whose aid they would come to depend on, was Keninya, promptly nicknamed "Joe." He told them through sign language that they were down near Cambridge Bay, a destination not on their route, and that the Bathurst post was about four hours away by boat. The men calculated that they had enough gas to make the post if they combined the remaining fuel from the two planes.

Colonel MacAlpine decided that the Western Canada Airways 'SK should make the trip without further delay. With 'SP already a write-off, this plane would be more likely to return safely. Finances could also have been a factor, since WCA leased out their aircraft for $1.75 per mile plus a charge of $75 per day, and Domex had already gone beyond their intended time frame.[11] There were further discussions about northwest headwinds, which would make flying difficult and increase gas consumption considerably, but they decided to fly 'SK anyway, despite these concerns.

September 12–13, 1929
Richard Pearce's Diary, Arctic Coast

SK warmed up and taxied out in the morning, but trouble again, developed in the carburetor intake, so SK came in. All but 9½ gallons of gas had been used. This was transferred back into AO, and with good visibility, she started off with MacMillan, Milne, Baker, and Joe on board. They returned a few minutes later after finding it impossible to make the crossing of the sea. A conference was held and it was decided that it was best to [stay put and] prepare at once for winter, rather than chance a trip before freeze-up.

It was decided that Major Baker who was on his way to Bathurst to take charge of Dominion Explorers base there, would be in charge of the party, and in case of differences of opinions that Col. MacAlpine would be final arbitrator. All of us realized our position, but morale was good. The chief worry was not personal inconvenience, but home conditions and anxiety that would be caused our families. Joe brought more salmon, and we are becoming used to it.

The situation of the prospectors could now be seen for what it was — very grim. They were above the Arctic Circle with no gas, very little food, inadequate clothing, and on floats that would soon be rendered useless by freeze-up. They were also uncomfortably aware that MacAlpine's direct instructions to Domex had been to hold off on any search, if they did not reach their predetermined destinations, until September 18, which was nearly a week away.

Communications of the era were still primitive. At that time, there were only three or four wireless radio stations throughout the Canadian Barrens, one of which was at Bathurst Inlet. Ironically, the front page of *The Northern Miner*, September 26, 1929, reported that the new wireless station at Bathurst was not working. It had been shipped by the Canadian Marconi Company, and the set was incomplete. In addition, there had been an acid spillage from the batteries during shipping. This meant that no word could be sent of the MacAlpine expedition's failure to arrive at this base.

The sod house was built using permafrost soil, which unfortunately defrosted when the stove was lit. Although the walls kept out the harsh winds that blew, the dampness within the house made it unpleasant. But it was "home" to the Dominion Explorers.

Dusk arrived surreptitiously and darkness descended, sending the men with their thoughts either to the tent or their planes for another night of restless sleep. When they awoke, cramped and shivering, it became clear they would need better shelter, so they began building a sod house.

This project was a welcome distraction from the monotonous wait for freeze-up, but the work was no simple task. The soil was shallow and frozen, and the friable sod crumbled through their cold-stiffened fingers when they picked it up. The men had to scavenge far afield to locate materials, and it took almost a week to build the walls, which measured a twelve by fourteen feet area and were three feet thick to keep out the Arctic blasts. The dampness inside the sod house made for uncomfortable living quarters, but, nonetheless, the Domex men greeted each day as it came and continued about their daily task of building the house. It was believed that once the temperatures dropped, the sod walls would freeze and the dampness would subside.

September 15, 1929
Richard Pearce's Diary, Dease Point

This has been a tiring day for all of us, carrying frozen sod for the mud house and gathering fuel. Eight or nine hours' hard going and only two scanty meals, could hardly be considered a satisfactory day. The latest Eskimo arrival, whom we have named Jack, reiterated what Joe has told us about the impossibility of making the post now.... We offered a whaleboat and a big store of supplies if he would take out a message, an offer which he refused. We are now satisfied that the Eskimo will take us out when travelling is possible, and not before. Our new Eskimos showed Mac [MacMillan] a four-gallon can of gas in his cache, but says there is no more in the neighbourhood. He also told us there was no gas nor any supplies at Ellice River.

Since their initial plan to use the wings of 'AO as the roof proved to be impossible, one of the Inuit women sewed two canvas tarpaulins together for that purpose. Pontoon struts were taken from 'AO for use as a ridgepole. They also used a window from the aircraft to let in the light. To maintain warmth within their Arctic home they made the doorway small. So small, in fact, that they had to crawl to get in — not an easy task for the heftier members of the expedition! Against this door they erected a seven-by-eight-foot tent to serve as a buffer against the wind as well as provide space for food storage.

Lacking proper clothing and with limited knowledge of surviving in the North for an extended period of time, the Domex men believed that their best chance lay in their nearly completed shelter, guidance from the Inuit, and, ultimately, rescue. Tasks were assigned, and each man was given a duty to perform while they waited. It never occurred to them that they might fail to return home.

September 16, 1929
Richard Pearce's Diary, Dease Point

We had to lay off house building to gather more fuel. We are going very slow on the grub [6.5 ounces of food per person each day] and everyone is hungry. Boadway lent me an extra pair of pants today. When we came here they wouldn't go around the waist; now they are loose. The rest of the party is in about the same shape; all losing weight rapidly... There has been speculative talk in idle moments as to whether the Bathurst wireless station is working. If it is, we hope an alarm has been sent out and planes will soon be looking for us.

Thus began the wait for 4°C, the optimum temperature at which water molecules begin to form ice.

| Two |

Preparations for the Search

First and most important care is that of one's body, so "clothing" will receive primary consideration. Pack in your kit the heaviest possible woollen socks, lumberjack's stockings, felt insoles, duffels, moose skin moccasins or mukluks, a pair of low rubbers to cover the moccasins when necessary ... ALWAYS KEEP YOUR FEET DRY.

... If circumstances arise under which you cannot help getting the footgear wet, such as when walking through overflow or water on top of ice, dip your feet quickly in and out of the water and let the water freeze on the outside of your footgear. Keep doing this until you have a good coating of ice all over your moccasins. When you have a good thick coat of ice on your feet, get through the overflow as quickly as possible... Overflows have caused many frozen feet in the North.

From "Northern Survival Techniques for Western Canada Airways Novice Pilots," September 23, 1929, Andy Cruickshank's teaching material, Prince George, British Columbia.

On September 23, Andy Cruickshank's phone rang. He was the superintendent of Western Canada Airways (WCA) in Prince George, British Columbia. The caller was Leigh Brintnell, his boss and the head of WCA's field force.[1] Cruickshank had been following the news reports about the missing Domex group and knew they had not arrived at Bathurst Inlet. He also knew that Western Canada Airways was already low on aircraft, having leased two planes to Domex, the ruined 'SP and 'SK replacement. Cruickshank expected that a search would be underway quickly because the cessation of float-plane flying period was imminent, and timing would be critical. This time in the calendar year was known to pilots as the in-between season, which literally meant the time between the end of float season and the beginning of ski flying. It could be a matter of a few days before the waterways froze sufficiently for ski landings, or it could take weeks.

Brintnell wasted no time in giving Cruickshank his instructions. They were simple — find the missing men and bring them back safely. Cruickshank would be in charge of the pilots, planes, and search routes during the search, and Guy Blanchet, a Dominion Explorers field worker, would be responsible for ensuring the well-being of the expedition members.

Cruickshank put his office in order and left for home to prepare for the search. Alf Walker, his mechanic, was busy overhauling G-CASQ, a Fokker Super Universal, for the flight out, and the two agreed to meet back at the Prince George hangar with their kits as soon as possible.

The media continued daily reports about the missing Dominion Explorers. Mr. McDougall, the treasurer of Domex, gave a statement on September 23, 1929, to *The Manitoba Free Press* that instructions had been given for the commencement of an

Karram Family Collection.

Cruickshank, shown here in his serge, joined the Royal Canadian Mounted Police in April 1923. The charismatic officer rode in the RCMP "gymkhana" while posted at Vancouver's "E" division, where he monitored immigration at the Port of Vancouver.

intensive search: "The relief planes detailed to fly into Mackenzie River territory at dawn this morning will be piloted by 'Punch' Dickens [*sic*] and Andy Cruickshanks [*sic*]. Both have had much experience in flying in the great northwest."

Cruickshank had an international reputation as one of the world's finest pilots[2]; not only was his flying exemplary, but his knowledge of the North was encyclopedic. He had learned to fly the hard way, in the skies over France during the First World War. After the Great War, he emigrated from England to Canada and was one of only twelve recruits chosen to join the prestigious Royal Canadian Mounted Police (RCMP) in 1923.[3] After his first posting in Vancouver's "E" division he requested a transfer to Dawson, Yukon Territories, where his thirst for adventure would be fulfilled. It was in the North that he found his true home. He was later described in the *Western Canada Airways Bulletin* as one whom, "in the great spaces of the North had communed with Nature in all her moods, sifted the essentials, and freed his soul from the trammels of dogma."[4] He was awestruck by its remorseless beauty and developed a high regard for and a lasting friendship with the local Aboriginal people.

His RCMP duties ranged from recording mining claims and land titles to collecting customs duties and acting variously as a coroner, Indian agent, health officer, tax collector, magistrate, jailer, and even guard for the Dawson banks. He went on patrols with dog teams, camping for weeks at a time as he journeyed from one settlement to another, often transporting the sick for miles to the nearest hospital. In the North he learned survival skills and with them a great respect for the forces of nature.

Cruickshank left the RCMP in 1927 and set up the Yukon Airways and Transportation Company with James Finnegan and Clyde Wann. He lobbied the Yukon and Dominion governments for permission to fly commercial flights and airmail in the North. Once this request was granted he ordered a Ryan M-2 monoplane to carry the mail and begin commercial flying. But just prior to completion of the aircraft Cruickshank was approached by

Karram Family Collection

Cruickshank met Esmé Trevor-Bulkley while hiking in Capilano Canyon, North Vancouver. At that time, RCMP officers were not permitted to marry unless they had served with the force for five years. Cruickshank bought his release from the Mounties and married Esmé in 1927. The couple flew with Charles Lindbergh and his wife Anne in 1928.

Charles Lindbergh, who asked if he could take delivery of the plane instead, since he was vying for a prize for the first non-stop flight across the Atlantic. The $25,000 prize, offered in 1919 by New York hotelier Raymond Orteig, was for the first aviator to make a non-stop flight from either Paris to New York or New York to Paris. Cruickshank agreed to give up his position in line for the Ryan, and while he waited for the next plane in production, Lindbergh made his historic flight on the plane named *The Spirit of St. Louis.*[5] This flight proved pivotal, since it demonstrated that a stock engine could run continuously for 33.5 hours. Engines like this could withstand the rigours of the North.

In that same year Cruickshank married Esmé Trevor-Bulkley. They set sail from Vancouver to Skagway with Cruickshank's dismantled aircraft aboard the ship. Soon after, he began his career as a northern bush pilot flying the reassembled *Queen of the Yukon.*

Cruickshank (or Chief Thunderbird as he would soon be known to the local Aboriginal people) quickly gained an impressive understanding of the equinoctial weather systems in the North, grasping the impact of the wind currents that formed high above the Arctic Circle, sending fog and low clouds to the flat landscape of the Northwest Territories. He became well acquainted with the updrafts and whirlwinds that were generated by the mountainous regions in the Yukon. While living in the North he learned firsthand that everything needed for survival was there, provided that one was attuned to the environment.

In 1929, the Northwest Territories was approximately 1.3 million square miles, so to search for two planes and eight men in such a vast area was an enormous, nearly impossible task. However, his knowledge and experience made him the obvious choice to be placed in charge of directing the aerial search, and he accepted his assignment with determination and resolve. Nevertheless, it wasn't easy for him to embark on a journey that would separate him from Esmé and their eight-month-old daughter Dawn for an indefinite period of time. Their home was a one-room cabin, the size of a garden shed, measuring a mere ten-by-twelve feet. It was presided over by Esmé, a woman of incredible strength, whose sense of adventure matched that of her husband. She had been taken on many flights throughout the Yukon, Alaska, and British Columbia. In fact, she was credited with delivering the first airmail into Dawson in November 1927, having pushed the mailbag out of the plane window as her husband lined up a flight path down the main street of the town. While she flew with him, Cruickshank was training his wife to become a pilot.

Karram Family Collection.

The Cruickshank family, Andy, Esmé, and baby Dawn, are enjoying a moment of sunshine in front of their Prince George cabin just days before Cruickshank left for the Arctic.

Esmé completely understood the task her husband had been assigned and immediately began assembling his kit. Using the same list that he had outlined for his young pilots, she laid out woollen underwear, heavy serge and mackinaw breeches, a mackinaw, a buckskin shirt, a heavy woollen sweater, a caribou parka and pants, several pairs of woollen mitts (as well as moose-skin mitts to put over the woollen mitts), and 15 cent gloves for plane repairs.

Although she had the utmost confidence in her spouse, she knew the hazards of the in-between season in the North only too well — that the area would soon become a stark, seemingly dead world, animated only by the sound of the shrieking wind. Though she kept her qualms to herself, she could not help but wonder what lay in store, not only for her husband, but also for the other men on the search who had their own families. An hour or so later she heard the drone of Cruickshank's plane as he made his customary pass overhead and watched as he dipped his wings in farewell. On this day, her eyes followed his aircraft as he headed into the clouds. Her heart was heavy.

The Northern Miner, on September 26, 1929, ran the story that Cruickshank's instructions, issued by Leigh Brintnell, had been to fly with Alf Walker to Fort McMurray then on to Fitzgerald and the Coronation Gulf, where he would meet Clennell H. "Punch" Dickins on that day. From there they would head to Stony Rapids.

What should have been two days' travel for Cruickshank and Walker turned into a nightmarish week. Almost immediately after takeoff they ran into bad weather that forced them down at Hudson Hope, where they remained all day. The following morning they doggedly pushed on, but soon encountered heavy rains, forcing them to land on the Peace River. They were finally able to lift off in the evening and managed to reach Peace River Crossing in spite of the rain, sleet, and snow. Despite the freezing temperatures, the water was not frozen, and Cruickshank landed safely, without damaging the floats on the plane.

September 26, 1929
Andy Cruickshank's Diary, Peace River Crossing

Flew to McMurray and [tried to go] on to
Fitzgerald. Bucked a 50 mile gale on Slave River,
ran out of gas, forced to land. Wind blew us
upstream one and a half miles before we could
get ashore. Found a small cabin, No. 10 Buffalo
Camp, tied machine safely and stayed overnight.

After their standard breakfast of fried bacon, bannock, tea, and
half-frozen pears, Walker and Cruickshank each perched on one of
the plane's floats and, wielding paddles, attempted to paddle the
twenty miles to Fitzgerald. But a strong wind whipped up waves,
making any forward progress impossible. Finally, the pair decided
to turn the aircraft around and they paddled it back to shore where
they secured it again. They then began trekking downstream. In his
diary entry for September 27, 1929, Andy wrote: "Walked down
river 10 miles to Fitzgerald. Walker got stuck in quicksand. [He]
was wearing waders. By using lots of driftwood I made a platform
and got him out of his boots."

It took the strength of both men, lying on the platform, to pull
Walker's boots out of the mire, one at a time. They trudged onward,
eventually finding a Native camp where they borrowed a canoe.
After making their way upriver, they tied the plane to the canoe
to tow the aircraft to Fitzgerald. This proved equally impossible.
Once again they turned around, paddled upstream, secured the
plane onshore, and spent the second night in cabin number ten.

At daybreak Cruickshank and Walker paddled to Fitzgerald, left
the canoe, bought gas, and borrowed a powerboat to take them back
to 'SQ. After refuelling the plane they set off again, heading towards
Fitzgerald and their rendezvous with Dickins. However, when they
landed they found that Dickins had already left. Dickins had flown
with MacAlpine and Pearce during the summer of 1928 to drop off

prospectors and visit some of the Domex bases, so he was familiar with the area and had a personal connection to the lost party. He covered roughly 2,600 miles on flights through rain, fog, snow, and high winds but found no sign of the missing planes or the men. He then returned to his normal posting with Western Canada Airways.

When they reached Fitzgerald, Cruickshank and Walker were asked to fly to the Domex camp at Stony Rapids, on the easterly shore of Lake Athabasca, where primary search planes with pilots and mechanics were waiting for further direction. Two planes were waiting for Cruickshank at Stony Rapids, and two more were standing by at Baker Lake. The roster of this search and rescue team was outstanding. Flying a Fokker Super Universal (G-CASO) with mechanic Paul Davis was Roy Brown, a First World War veteran. "Bertie" Hollick-Kenyon, a young pilot and another First

Right: Francis Roy Brown lived in Winnipeg until the outbreak of the First World War. He enlisted in the Canadian Cycle Corps and was sent to France where he served at Ypres, Vimy, and Passehendaele. Left: Bill Spence, smoking his trademark pipe, poses next to a set of caribou antlers at Bathurst Inlet. Born in 1892 in Oshawa, Ontario, Spence acted as chief pilot for Dominion Explorers.

World War veteran, with mechanic Bill Nadin, flew a Fokker Super Universal (G-CASL). Bill Spence of Dominion Explorers flew with mechanic E.G. Longley and Guy Blanchet, a Domex northern surveyor, aboard a Fairchild CF-ACZ. Jim D. Vance from Northern Aerial Minerals Exploration, with mechanic B.C. Blasdale assisting, also flew a Fokker Super Universal (G-CARK). Thankfully, a wireless system linked Baker Lake and Stony Rapids, which meant that critical decisions and plans could be made.

The Manitoba Free Press, September 25, 1929, detailed the area of the proposed search:

> Tentative plans for the aerial hunt for the McAlpine [*sic*] mining party missing in the sub-arctic revolves about one of the most forsaken areas in the Northwest Territories, namely, the region between Bathurst Inlet and Coronation ... That country is declared to be about the most hazardous hop in the 2,000-mile journey from Baker to Aklavik ... on account of the

G-CARK, the Fokker Super Universal, owned by Northern Aerial Minerals Exploration, is readied for the search. The 'RK was the first Super Universal to be made by Fokker and was purchased by president John Hammell.

extreme dangers of using seaplanes in the far
north so late in the season, most of the rescue
planes will likely carry ski equipment so that the
undercarriage may be changed to suit conditions
beyond the 65th parallel ... But even with winter
equipment on board, the pilots who are joining
the widespread rescue trek are fully aware of the
fact thate [*sic*] they are daring death by venturing
into the sub-Arctic with pontoon machines so
late in the year....

Further stories heralded that the "Mighty Air Fleet" would
be based out of Stony Rapids. The report continued that this
would be the greatest air hunt in history and the airmen would
comb the sub-Arctic in search of the Dominion Explorers that
had been lost for weeks.

September 18, 1929
Richard Pearce's Diary, Dease Point

The boys are talking about the probability of a
plane coming in here for it is pretty well agreed
a search for us is now on. Everyone on the party
feels keenly our helplessness and inability to
move toward a post at this time. Joe told us
again to-night by illustration a canoe would be
swamped, and I guess he is right. At any rate,
the Colonel is positive that no one take a chance
on a move that the Eskimos will not take part
in, though all of us have offered to do so, if he
would give his consent.

While Andy Cruickshank and Alf Walker had been fighting
their way north, gas and supplies were already being freighted up

the Dubawnt River to Wholdaia and Dubawnt Lakes under highly adverse weather conditions. It was important to cache supplies along the projected search routes as there were weight and capacity restrictions for the Fokkers and Fairchilds. These supplies enabled the search planes to refuel and extend their searches further afield without having to return to the home base each day.

Roy Brown and Bill Spence had also run quick searches from Baker Lake on the 26th and 27th and discovered that the supply cache at Beverly Lake had been emptied. This was the first encouraging sign that the MacAlpine group had made it into the sub-Arctic. From Beverly Lake, Spence and Brown flew on to Baker Lake to await Cruickshank's arrival and instructions. But Cruickshank and his team, operating from Stony Rapids, were in the process of making fuel and supply caches, and would not reach them for a number of days. During this time, a major concern had become apparent. Only Cruickshank and Walker in 'SQ, Hollick-Kenyon and Nadin in 'SL, and Vance and Blasdale in 'RK were carrying skis in preparation for freeze-up.[6]

The other two planes needed to be equipped with these essentials as soon as possible, prompting Cruickshank to contact the RCMP and request that equipment be sent upriver by boat to Baker Lake. Despite apprehensions about the forthcoming unpredictable weather and the large area in which they needed to search, optimism remained high that the MacAlpine group was safe somewhere north of Beverly Lake and that the rescue teams would find them and bring them out quickly.

Optimism for the Dominion Explorers was starting to wane. Without gas for the planes or safe conditions for boat travel, the Domex group's only means of travel once freeze-up occurred would be on foot, and this would be tough going.

A reporter from *The Northern Miner* had every confidence that the men were amply prepared to face the unpredictable weather conditions:

A certain amount of fur clothing was taken aboard
the two MacAlpine planes at Baker Lake, and if
the party has shot caribou as is quite likely, they
will have fashioned some rude protection against
the weather from the hides. The country abounds
in ptarmigan and arctic hare, both being easily
caught or trapped. They were supplied with fish
net and lines, and so long as they could cut holes
through the frozen lakes they could catch fish,
which are fairly plentiful ... It has been a fairly
open and mild fall in the Barren lands, according
to Mr. Blanchet (explorer and navigator of
Dominion Explorers Limited), whose experience
of that country is as great as that of most men.

In fact, the expedition members had not taken any winter
clothing from the post at Baker Lake and so would not enjoy the
warmth of fur clothing. They had not landed on a lake so they
could not use their fishing lines, and ptarmigan would soon be
migrating south from the Arctic coast. Ptarmigan, a member of the
grouse family, were easily killed with a stone and would be good
eating for the hungry men. Although these fat, fuzzy birds adapted
well to the harsh Arctic climate, they did move from the higher
latitudes to escape the darkness of the winter months. Footwear
posed a further challenge for the Domex crew, as few of the men
were suitably outfitted for the region. What little they had was
supplied by the ever-helpful Inuit, but there was not enough to go
around (and it didn't always fit very well).

Their food supplies were also dwindling, with no end to their
confinement in sight. They were down to twenty-five pounds of
flour, one-and-a-half tins of baking soda, half a pound of lard,
a small tin of pork and beans, two-and-a-half tins of milk, four
ounces of jam, a pound of salt, two ounces of pepper, two pounds
of apricots, ten pounds of beans, half-a-pound each of rice and

tea, two-and-a-half pounds of raisins, three tins of Frey Bentons corned beef, four pounds of sugar, two pounds of currants, one tin each of tomatoes and sausages, a bottle of coffee, a package of dates, half a dozen hardtack biscuits, a package of mushroom soup, twenty-eight chocolate bars, and thirty bouillon cubes. This standard bush fare was heavy on the carbohydrates but noticeably lacking in protein, fat, and fresh produce. Bush fare was fine for a short period of time, but by now the Domex men were feeling the effects of vitamin deficiencies, and day to day work was becoming physically draining.

The stranded men continued their chores around camp — finding and cooking food, gathering fuel and shoring up their frequently collapsing sod house. To supplement their food stores, they hunted the increasingly elusive ptarmigan, along with ground squirrel and ducks, and landed the occasional fish. The Inuit were generous with their own food, mostly whitefish, dried salmon, and the occasional bits of caribou, sometimes green in colour — a sign of the meat's advanced age and almost always indigestible to the Domex men. Major Baker had an additional challenge in eating — a badly infected tooth, which he was treating (inadequately) with Mercurochrome. The lack of fresh fruit and vegetables was beginning to take its toll, and despite bursts of energy, the men were weakening. A vitamin C deficiency weakens blood vessels and can cause a general malaise characterized by lack of enthusiasm.

Initially, the cooking of their meagre food supplies was done on a stove made from one of the plane's heaters, but the men were grateful when MacMillan traded a pair of field glasses for a more functional cooker. The Inuit explained to the men how to use moss and bits of scrub to fuel it. One evening, dinner consisted of grebes, water birds that the men called "hell-divers." The oily meat left a layer of grease in the pot, and the meal made them so queasy that they decided to settle their stomachs with a tot of rum. In the dark, someone inadvertently used the water from the dishpan to mix with the alcohol. This did little for the flavour of the liquor, and MacAlpine asked for hot water to help wash it down. He was accidentally given straight dishwater, gulped it down, and promptly vomited. To commemorate this event they dubbed their location Dishwater Point.

Pearce kept up his diary entries, summarizing each day as it came. To keep themselves occupied, the men played bridge with a deck of cards that Goodwin had made from linen maps. Baker decided the men needed to build up their strength for the trek to Cambridge Bay, so they went hiking along the shoreline, all the while hunting for food and observing the ice conditions, which unfortunately never seemed to change. Pearce even took on the task of surgeon and lanced the abscess in Baker's mouth. Meanwhile, their sod hut continued to bulge and buckle in the warm temperatures.

Only eight hundred miles from one another, a day's plane journey apart, both searchers and expedition members were impatiently waiting for the same thing. Until freeze-up, progress by air and on foot would be impossible.

| THREE |

Grounded by Weather

September 28, 1929
Richard Pearce's Diary Dease Point

*A queer bright arch, like a white bow, showed in the sky to the
north for several hours. None of us have ever seen anything like
it before. Little new ice formed on the sea overnight, but the
lake from which we get our fresh water has at least six inches.*

The days to the men stretched endlessly and although they kept
busy doing daily chores, their minds continually wandered to the
thought of rescue and if an attempt would be successful. They
knew twenty days had elapsed since they had been heard from.

Cruickshank and his search team were gravely concerned
about the waterways because a freeze was imminent. Once this

happened rescue attempts would have to be abandoned until the lakes were sufficiently frozen to withstand the weight of an aircraft on skis.

For the next few days the flyers raced against time, freighting drums filled with fuel from Stony Rapids to Wholdaia Lake. They placed gas and provisions at another small lake on the plateau near Wholdaia, where lower temperatures would cause ice to form more quickly and enable their fully loaded ski planes to take off safely. The preferred supply route was north along the course of the Dubawnt River and Lake to Wholdaia Lake, 280 miles southeast of Fort Reliance. The weather, although adverse, still permitted flights and supplies were being cached for later transfer.

These preparations, while necessary, were also frustrating since they further diverted the pilots from their purpose. They had come to search for the lost expedition, but could not do this until sufficient supplies had been cached before freeze up. After careful consideration, Cruickshank, Vance, and Hollick-Kenyon, along with the mechanics, decided to fly to Baker Lake (140 miles to the east of Wholdaia) and check on the status of supplies at the next search base.

Tommy Siers, along with Pat Semple, had been directed by Brintnell to head to Cranberry Portage via rail. They would then be flown to Stony Rapids to meet up with Cruickshank, Hollick-Kenyon, and Vance. Siers would be head mechanic for the searchers. His expertise and innovation regarding aircraft maintenance and repair would prove to be invaluable. Cruickshank bantered and joked at great length with Semple, an Irishman and an air engineer with Western Canada Airways. Once they were all together, the men boarded the planes and headed for Baker Lake, with hopes that the lakes would not yet be frozen over.

Even though all three planes carried skis, a forced float landing on a partially frozen lake so late in the season could mean disaster. Also of concern was the fact that if the temperature dropped overnight, the planes would be embedded in ice. Snow squalls

Three aircraft on the shores of Baker Lake in October 1929 wait for freeze-up.

hampered visibility and made their flight extremely treacherous. Dropping lower to avoid cloud, the three pilots were dismayed to see that all small lakes were iced over, signalling the beginning of freeze-up. Luckily the larger open water lakes, including Baker, still allowed safe float plane landings.

At Baker Lake they discovered that Brown and Spence had not been able to do as many search runs as hoped for because of fuel shortages. They also found that supplies were dismally inadequate. After conferring with them and Guy Blanchet, Cruickshank decided that he and the others would return to Stony Rapids via Wholdaia Lake to continue freighting supplies. During the flight, the weather turned on them with clouds, mist, and rain, reducing visibility and forcing them to set up camp at Wholdaia for the night and wait it out.

While the air engineers tended to the aircraft, Cruickshank got out the frying pans to make bannock, a staple food in the bush. He mixed flour with water and formed the dough. Then he fitted one frying pan over the other, creating a sort of oven. He placed the "oven" over the open sputtering fire, which then captured and retained the heat and the dough baked. He cooked up some beans and meat and the men sat down in the tent to enjoy a nice hot dinner. Walker, however, broke a tooth during dinner, which he claimed was a victim of Cruickshank's bannock. They finished off their meal with tea, which was the proven stimulant in the bush, as it "went further" than coffee.

The group settled down to wait out the storm that was raging outside, thankful for being inside a tent that did not leak. Cruickshank and Semple were both inveterate tellers of remarkable tales, and Semple guffawed at every yarn Cruickshank spun, hooting his disbelief at each opportunity. The evening passed in a jovial manner and in relative comfort, and they finally separated into their tents and drifted off to sleep.

The Manitoba Free Press gave an updated report from Thayer Lindsley on September 30, saying that no word had been received from the planes scanning the rocky Barren Lands but the search was being "prosecuted with vigour." Lindsley also stated that the pilots were "howling for gas."

Then, during the night of October 1, near disaster struck. One of the mechanics approached Bill Nadin and Hollick-Kenyon that morning and calmly said, "Your aircraft has sunk."

Nadin replied, "Don't be daft."

The bearer of the news answered, "Take a walk down and have a look for yourself."[1]

Although 'SL's fuselage was completely submerged, the front end of the plane was held above the water's surface by a rope attached to the stump of a rotten tree. The plane had been loaded the previous day with drums of fuel, and, although the aircraft was thought to be secure, the wind had changed direction during the night, creating a problem for 'SL. Water receded, causing the tail to dip, which, in turn, allowed water to seep into the rear end of the floats, gradually filling them and causing the plane to sink tail-first. It was salvaged, repaired, inspected, and passed airworthy by Semple, and, once weather permitted, it continued to fly provisions along with 'SQ and 'RK to Wholdaia Lakes during the daylight hours.[2] Cruickshank stayed in touch with Spence and Brown, using the wireless, and kept them informed of the progress that was being made, which wasn't much.

On October 3, Cruickshank, Hollick-Kenyon, Vance, and all the mechanics left the base at Stony and flew to Wholdaia with the expectation of continuing to Baker Lake. However, snow squalls blew up, and again the pilots and their crew were forced to remain at Wholdaia and wait for a break in the weather. That meant that they were grounded without communication. The search preparations had come to a complete stop.

———

September 29, 1929
Richard Pearce's Diary, Dease Point

We got an awful shock to wake up during the early morning to hear rain beating on the roof of the mud shack. As the roof is flat, it soon started to bulge and drip water. The side of the shack Tom and I sleep on got the worst of it, and we had to get up. It made the day longer than usual. But worse still, it took snow and frost out of the shack walls, and we had to put on more rope braces ... Our Eskimo friends broke camp and went to the west, apparently to the same place that Charlie and Jack left for a few days ago to bring fish.

Things were not going well at the Domex camp. Morale was sinking and the men's stomachs were reacting to the food they were compelled to eat, prompting Pearce to comment, "They say hunger will make one like anything, but I don't believe it yet."[3] The fish the

Inuit had left them were turning mouldy, and their own supplies were dwindling rapidly, even though they had reduced their meals to two a day. One of the men brought in some ground squirrel, but Pearce couldn't bring himself to cook it.

Along with the physical deterioration, it seemed that the psychological strain was beginning to show. Colonel MacAlpine decided that a statement should be drawn up in the event of their deaths. Major Baker wrote the document:

> In view of the tragedies, which have formerly occurred in the Barrens at this season of the year, first, last and all the time my first principle is absolute safety of personnel.
>
> We had three alternatives: (a) to remain here until we could travel over the ice on the gulf: (b) to try and get to the post by boat: or (c)

Provincial Archives of Manitoba, Canadian Air Lines Collection #2143.

Colonel Cyril MacAlpine stands next to "Joe" outside the tent that housed all their fuel — moss, twigs, lichen, and twisted willow. The tent served to keep it dry. Food is being air dried on a line between the two men, a method of preserving food in the absence of refrigeration. The process met with varying rates of success and was subject to "raids" from predators.

to move to a point nearer the post and try and signal same by flares.

As to (a): the difficulties in staying were food and protection against the weather. These difficulties I felt could be overcome, particularly with the friendly assistance of the Eskimos. As to (b): This was absolutely impossible, as the only means of transport was an unseaworthy canoe. The Eskimos, who knew the situation, ridiculed the idea of going themselves and indicated swamping in the sea.

As to (c): I did consider this alternative, using the Eskimo canoe, but they flatly refused to lend their boat and indicated the proposal foolhardy. At an earlier date in the season this alternative would have been feasible, but at this season of the year was too dangerous. The small lakes started to freeze the day after we landed and the ice formed in the sheltered bays of the sea coast and every few days we had blizzards, or ice-cold rains, until winter set in in earnest.

Without a boat we could not cross the rivers. Furthermore the party was ill equipped with clothing for any attempt of the kind. For part of the party to attempt same would mean a division of our scanty supply of food. The Eskimos also pointed out the Cambridge Post had high hills around it and signals from this side of the sea could not be observed.

Reluctantly, therefore, the only possible decision was, from the standpoint of safety of personnel, to do what we have done; namely, wait until we could travel over the ice.

With the Inuit gone, the Domex people sank further into gloom. Aboriginal people were the lifeline that connected MacAlpine and his men not only to the land and survival in the Barrens, but kept alive their hopes for a safe trek across Dease Strait to Cambridge Bay. The Domex group of eight had some experience of Arctic conditions, but they were human and as susceptible to anxiety and despair as anyone else. The cold and hunger did not help either. The following day Colonel MacAlpine wrote his own statement, to which all members of the group "subscribed and agreed."[4]

MacAlpine's statement was a detailed report on the events that led up to the forced stay at Dease Point. He wrote that it was the late arrival of WCA's 'SK that was at the root of the problem. He determined that eleven days had elapsed between the sinking of 'SP and the arrival of 'SK. Those days had been perfect for flying but instead were spent waiting. In fact, under ideal conditions they could have nearly completed their expedition and returned to Winnipeg. MacAlpine also detailed the flying and weather conditions once the flights continued, stressing that the weather was deteriorating and small lakes were beginning to freeze over. His report gave the reasons why the planes had flown off course and why they reached the decision to remain at Dease Point with the Inuit and wait for either rescue or good conditions to walk out.[5]

By October 2 Pearce had no choice but to cook up the formerly rejected ground squirrels. The water used to cook the meat was quite greasy, and, as Pearce was about to throw it out, a "holler went up and it was saved. Grease a quarter inch thick came to the top of the water when it cooled. I suppose it is merely a matter of how hungry one is, to make any grub good."[6]

Keeping busy was crucial. The hunters went in search of food, and the fuel gatherers scrounged for anything that would burn. On one particular day, the weather changed, sending wind-whipped snow around the working men, giving them hope that a freeze was upon them, but then the snow changed to sleet, and they ran for cover in the sod house. The roof began to leak in earnest, and their hopes of a good snowfall and cold snap were dashed. Both Thompson and Pearce stayed up all night, emptying the pots and pans they used to catch the drips from the roof.

October 3, 1929
Richard Pearce's Diary, Dease Point

It is another rotten day, with the wind switching from the south to northeast, and driving an icy rain ... It is a double birthday in the party, Mac being 29 and Don 26. They had an extra portion of fish this morning to celebrate the occasion. When I wished Don many happy returns, he said, "Not here, I hope?" ... If some of the Arctic explorers could hear the remarks passed about them here they would be far from pleased, for instance, we were told that we could expect the freeze-up in this section about the 19th or 20th of September. Ice-making on the sea is much slower than we expected.

Back at Wholdaia Lake, the search team was also concerned about the uncertainty of the weather. They needed clear skies for flying, and the snow that kept them from going back to Baker Lake had also created problems for the tug *Ocean Eagle* that was bringing the skis for 'CZ and 'SO and more fuel to Baker Lake. To make matters worse, a radio check to confirm supplies determined that some of the vital equipment was not on board.[7] The tug then had to make its way back through the churning waves to Churchill to retrieve the missing equipment. The days passed with no sign of the tug's arrival at Baker Lake, and, since the boat had no wireless, Blanchet flew with Spence to look for it. Finally they spotted her, encrusted with ice, barely managing to advance through strong northwest gales.[8] All they could do was watch helplessly from the air, then turn back to their base. It seemed no matter how well thought out the plan was, the forces of nature had something else in mind.

Cruickshank managed to fly to Stony Rapids for messages and heard about the problem with the *Ocean Eagle* and the barge that accompanied it. When he and Alf Walker then tried to get back to Wholdaia, they were met with a fifty-foot ceiling and quarter-mile visibility, so they turned the plane around. They were, however, able to send messages to Baker Lake, and planned for a direct flight once the weather permitted. The men settled at Stony to wait for fairer skies.

The tug finally made its way into Baker Lake on October 8 with Dr. Don Bruce, an RCMP constable, and supplies. With the assistance of a trader's schooner anchored at the Baker Lake trading post, Blanchet, Spence, and Brown met the tug and transferred the load.[9] The headlines of *The Manitoba Free Press*, October, 2, 1929, heralded the news of the intrepid airman and the progress of the desperate rescue attempt, detailing the dangers of the journey as the tug's captain turned and headed back down Chesterfield Inlet to the port in Churchill. Because this journey took place later in the year than had ever been attempted before, he faced the same difficulties as the pilots. It was touch and go as to whether the

The SS Ocean Eagle *en route from Port Fort Churchill to Baker Lake. Storms that frequently "blew up" in the vast Hudson Bay made travel exceedingly dangerous.*

ship would be able to make it to Churchill[10] before the waterway became completely frozen.

The newspaper continued with details about Dr. Don Bruce, who had been commissioned by Dominion Explorers to lend medical assistance when and if the missing men were found. He would also tend to any of the rescue team if needed. Dr. Bruce was well-suited to working in the North, having gained considerable experience with northern issues when, earlier that year, he had been instrumental in stemming a typhoid outbreak in northern Manitoba.

———

The front page of *The Manitoba Free Press* on October 8 declared that no word had yet been heard from Cruickshank, but expressed the hope that the reason for this was bad weather. However, unbeknownst to them, Cruickshank had made a successful attempt on the 8th to reach Wholdaia. From there, he and Walker flew on with Vance, their planes fully loaded, to Baker Lake, travelling 450 miles through snowstorms and finally landing on glassy water in a thick and blinding blizzard. This type of landing is one of the most difficult tasks that a pilot is asked to perform. The shiny flat surface distorts a pilot's depth perception so he cannot gage the height above the water. Hollick-Kenyon, rounding out the group, finally arrived later the same day. *The Northern Miner*, on October 10, 1929, gave the news to a captive audience that all five primary searchers were now together at Baker Lake with the necessary equipment and 7,000 gallons of fuel. It seemed like luck had finally turned in their favour.

However, luck did not appear to have been with the Domex men:

October 5, 1929
Richard Pearce's Diary, Dease Point

Our programme of two meals a day is not very inspiring; particularly as we are staying in bed until eleven in the morning to save fuel and are back into our sleeping bags again at eight. For breakfast to-morrow we are to have a cup of rice soup each and for the second meal two cups of ptarmigan stew. The ptarmigan are flocking and going south. Ducks, geese, swans and so forth have already gone.

The following day was the day the Inuit were due back. Their failure to appear was a devastating blow to the Domex men and the strain was almost more than any of them could bear. It began to show in alarming ways. While hunting, Pearce suddenly became very lethargic and had to be helped back to camp, though he managed to perk up after a "slug of Scotch."[11] Colonel MacAlpine wasn't faring well, either. He had tightened his belt by sixteen inches since arriving at Dease Point. Talk of the tentative departure date to Cambridge Bay created tension among the men, and the colonel had to intervene. "… [T]his patient waiting stuff is the bunk,"[12] Pearce complained. To boost their spirits and to pull everyone together again, chocolate bars were doled out.

The men settled in for the night, after moving Thompson and Pearce away from the leak in the tarpaulin. There were now eight men in a row along a ten-foot length. This made for a tight squeeze, but it also created warmth for them. The sod walls smelled of damp dirt, which just increased the sense of cold. The disintegrating, discoloured, and perpetually leaky tarpaulin bulged and stretched over their living space, and the window of 'AO was fogged up with the interior moisture. The damp and dank gloom permeated everything. Sleep was a welcome distraction from the almost unbearable situation.

Dawn arrived and thankfully the temperature outside had dropped. The men checked the stability of the ice and found it rubbery, yet it gave them hope. The snow had melted around Dease Point, which the Domex men thought might be the cause of the late return of the Inuit. Worry escalated, as their food supplies were getting perilously low. The Inuit had wind-dried the naturally oily whitefish, and, when the oil turned rancid, it gave the entire fish a rotten taste. Although the fish is still edible, to the European palates it is almost unpalatable. The dried fish, their main source of nourishment, were cached under piles of rock, and while this method of storage didn't do much for maintaining freshness, it did keep animals from raiding the food.

There was more arguing about whether to stay or go on October 9, but with some pushing to go and others urging caution to stay and wait for the Inuit, the men eventually agreed they couldn't take any decisive action unless they had three things: snow, strong ice, and the Inuit guides. While walking later that morning, Pearce and the colonel realized that the coastline was a labyrinth of islands and that trying to locate Cambridge Bay on their own would be foolish indeed. All the men were having a tough time keeping their minds busy and off of what might be happening "Outside," the term given to civilization by the bush pilots and explorers in the North. Pearce wrote, "… it is a real tough mental battle to keep control. This diary keeping is a godsend to me."[13]

By October 10, the Inuit had still not returned, adding to the bleakness of their days. To clear their heads, several went for a walk. MacAlpine and Pearce split from the group, but when they started back along the ice, the colonel broke through a few times and was badly soaked. The two men hurried back to the sod hut to warm up and dry out. "The rest of the boys went on over one of the islands and reported open water in the main channel, much to our disgust. That has taken some of the joy out of things, but we are still hopeful that the Eskimos know what they are talking about and that chances of our getting out soon are not dark."[14] The day ended on a high note, however, when Alex Milne made a discovery of half a package of wet cigarettes in 'AO. These were divided up, and Pearce remarked, "the butts were small, and the last I saw of Mac's was on the end of a fork. Bob gathered up all the remains and got an extra smoke."[15]

On the same day, the following headline appeared in *The Northern Miner*: "Winter Grips North and Stays Hands of Rescuers." The article went on to report that the sudden onset of freezing temperatures had halted the search flights on floats. All pilots and their crew were now grounded until the ice was strong enough to support the weight of the aircraft.

The air mechanics, under Siers' direction, began the preparations for winterizing 'SQ, 'SO, 'SL, 'RK, and 'CZ. The pilots taxied the planes to the shore on a very small sandy beach, in front of the Révillon Frères Trading Post.[16] Despite overcrowding,[17] they continued to work as nonchalantly as if they were comfortably back in Winnipeg hangars.

Since spare parts were non-existent and the mechanics had only basic tools, the engine components needed were made from whatever materials the men could scrounge. Stovepipes and sheet-iron metal were available, much to the delight of the mechanics. Firstly, the engine cowlings (the curved pieces of metal that cover and protect the engine) had to be winterized. This was done by closing off the openings that provided air access to cool the engine in the summer. A small shutter was fitted behind the propeller to close off the front of the engine, keeping out the frigid temperatures. All shutters were checked and secured.

Next, heaters were made for each plane, and although they did little in the freezing Arctic temperatures, they did work to some degree. The heat was achieved through an "Intensifier Tube" externally affixed to the end of the exhaust pipe. The heater unit itself was a little over thirty inches in length. It consisted of a long metal tube that provided an annulus around the exhaust pipe through which fresh air was heated. Using a control valve, hot air was delivered to the cabin.[18]

Then they began gathering the necessary components for the changeover from floats to skis. This was a major undertaking in the heated hangers in Winnipeg, let alone in the great outdoors of the North. Without the assistance of equipment the men would need to build a tree tripod and use a block and tackle to lift the 4,000 pound plane. Soon suitable trees were located, cut, and stripped. This extra work took precious time, but it was necessary for both the safety of the men working on the plane and for the integrity of the plane itself. All hands worked together to ensure that, once ready, the changeover would be smooth.

Although life in the North was anything but usual for the men, ordinary life went on in their hometowns. On October 14 Bill Nadin should have been in the throes of preparation for his wedding day. The talk naturally centered on Nadin's bride-to-be, and to ease the concern and disappointment, all the men showered Bill with rice.[19] Important dates came and went for both the marooned men and the rescue team.

October 11, 1929
Richard Pearce's Diary, Dease Point

This was the day we were supposed to start for Cambridge Bay. The thaw is no doubt responsible for the delay in the return of the Eskimos. This has gradually lowered the moral[e] of the party. We seem to be able to talk of nothing else. It tried to snow last night, then switched to rain for a while, but it is now colder again. Most of the boys are very pessimistic, although the Colonel sticks to his prophecy that we will leave by the 17th. I have a hunch he is saying this to keep up spirits. I couldn't make the grade with the whitefish again today. The first piece I got was bad; that seems to be my luck....

The situation was dismal. Human hopes can endure for only so long before the end of the rope is reached. The Domex men, who had started their expedition with enthusiasm and dreams of claiming nature's resources, had no dreams of riches now. They just wanted to go home, and that prospect began to seem less and less likely. The waiting was all-consuming. Waiting for food, waiting for ice, waiting for the Inuit, waiting for rescue.

Colonel MacAlpine decided that what the men needed was to get outside and walk again. So out they all went, cautiously trudging in their ill-fitting footwear over the uneven surface of the snow-covered ground and breathing the fresh, crisp air. They walked for about seven miles and, as they walked, the temperature began to drop, and this bolstered their morale. The fact that the colonel broke through the ice once more didn't dampen their spirits in the least.

October 11, 1929
Richard Pearce's Diary, Dease Point

Extra! — Charlie and his young brother, Jimmie, the Eskimos we had been waiting for, came in at six o'clock with their dog team. Were they welcome? I'll say they were. They brought part of a caribou and a lot of fish … I could only stand one helping, but the others had two. A full stomach once more; what a grand and glorious feeling.

The men's waning optimism almost instantly rebounded. The food was plentiful, the temperature was dropping, the ice was forming … all was good. Alex Milne celebrated his twenty-sixth birthday with a caribou feast and he said it was his most noteworthy birthday on record. After living for a month on five ounces of food per day each and then to have plenty was beyond their expectation. Preparations were now back on track for the trip to Cambridge Bay. With sufficient food intake, the colonel had the men begin to build up their strength for their sixty-mile trek for help.

What could possibly stop them now?

| FOUR |

Moving Northward

October 18, 1929
Richard Pearce's Diary, Dease Point

*Last night was an awful one. A real gale blew, probably up
to sixty miles an hour, driving the snow so that it felt like
bullets. Everything in the lean-to tents was covered and the
snow oozed through the cracks into the mud shack, making us
very uncomfortable. The tarpaulin roof split in several places
and we spent an anxious time while repairs were made. We
ran out of thread and were at our wits' ends until someone
hit on the happy idea of using surgical thread from the first
aid kit ... Jimmie stayed with us last night, crawling in with
Alex and Mac in their doubled-up sleeping bag. That made
nine of us in a row.*

The men's spirits sank like stones. The storm was a painful reminder of their precarious situation. The gale continued to blow during the day. Ice fragments crashed against the shoreline, obliterating the water's edge in blinding whiteness. One of the Inuit children had wandered into this howling gale, and Pearce joined in the desperate search for her. Caught in the wind, the five-year-old girl was swept perilously close to the shore. It was sheer luck that she was found before she was dragged in and drowned in the frigid surf.

Just when they thought things couldn't get any worse, the father of Jack, one of the Inuit, told the men he would be leaving for at least two days to get more fish for the trek out. Morale dropped even further with this news because the Inuit sense of time did not always correspond with theirs. The thought of another two days (or more) delay dampened what little hope the Domex men had of ever getting out of there. Their thoughts continually wandered to subjects "Outside."

Front page headlines of *The Northern Miner*, October 17, 1929, announced a story on their plight, "The Arctic Rescue Effort Boldly Begins Next Week." The paper continued to report that although the pilots were grounded due to weather conditions, the rescue team actively continued to plan their next moves. The two- and three-plane aerial searches would scour a three-hundred to four-hundred mile area between Baker Lake and Bathurst Inlet once the lakes had become frozen. This large area held the most promise of locating the missing men.

As Canadians gobbled up news of the missing expedition, optimism remained high that the men could survive in this land of eternal snow and ice. D.M. LeBourdais, Vilhjalmur Stefansson's biographer and Arctic companion, was quoted in *The Northern Miner* on October 10, 1929, as saying, "If there is one man with Arctic experience in the group he would see them through, but with all the men experienced and resourceful it is idle to worry about them." He continued with his thoughts of Stefansson's *The*

Friendly Arctic,[1] "It makes a great newspaper yarn, but I have no doubt the men are enjoying a splendid outing and hunting party. They should be able to live off the country and make themselves fairly comfortable for a very considerable period."

Members of the Dominion Explorers might have shaken their heads grimly at LeBourdais's blithe comments as they eked out the bare minimum for survival, depending both on the weather and the Inuit. At least their Inuit friends had finally returned with sleds and dog teams, indicating that the trek to Cambridge Bay would begin soon. But when? The violent storm destroyed the ice that had formed along the route they would be taking, once again postponing their departure. The mental strain from the wait was agony, and the men's hopes seemed as broken as the ice along the shore.

With the Inuit now numbering sixteen, Dishwater Point had become a crowded settlement with little to occupy the men's thoughts and actions. The waiting was all-consuming. Some gathered fuel. Others hunted for food. The colonel even made a list of the things the Inuit might want once the Domex men made their way to Cambridge Bay. They sang songs, told stories, and played cards — anything to distract them from the tedium of waiting.

Richard Pearce recorded his impressions of this time at Dease Point on October 19, 1929: "The storm blew itself out during the night and this is a beautiful day. I went outside early, and found that the snow had drifted right up to the top of the shack. The tent near the doorway had caved in, its steel ridgepole and end rods being broken. The drifts are as hard as rocks."

The men began their daily routine of shoring-up, propping-up, and cleaning-up. Pearce was invited to go by dog sled to a cache near Dishwater Point. He gladly hopped onboard with his Inuit friend Charlie, and when they reached their destination he was quite surprised to discover the real object of the journey was to distribute the belongings of an old woman who had recently died. Her "will" consisted of a single piece of paper with six rows of human figures drawn on it. Those gathered had all been invited to this ceremony and each came up and received their share of the woman's possessions, which ranged from a baking powder tin full of cigarette butts to a hand-sewing machine.

After the ceremony the group returned to their settlement, and around 3:00 in the afternoon the feasting began. Pearce managed to feed the group of twenty-four with the food that had been brought to camp from the cache. It was a very tight squeeze in the sod house, but the companionship seemed to calm the Domex men, or perhaps it was because the Inuit had given them a tentative date as to when they felt the ice would be ready to cross — or it could have been the fact that Pearce had been given some tobacco. The necessity to use toilet paper as cigarette rollers didn't damper the joyous event. At this gathering, forty days since they had first met, the men learned the Inuit names of their friends: "Grand-dad told me his name was Unani, that 'Mary's' was Helika, 'Jim's' Tepinna, 'Charlie's' wife, Bunnuck, 'Jack's' Awordiwo, 'Joe's' Keninya, 'Dad's' Otoogo, the pretty girl's Olga, and the new Eskimo, Tigattook, the mother Kena, 'Alice' Tigalook and 'Charlie' Penukta."[2]

The following morning, October 20, Mac wrote notices and placed them in both planes saying: "Everybody OK in party. Left here on October 21 with three huskie [sic] dog teams. It is planned that the Colonel, Pearce and Baker recuperate day or so at Cambridge, then proceed by dog team to Burnside base. If steamship Bay Maud is still wintering at Cambridge and her wireless is OK, then this trip to Burnside may not be necessary. If you have gas, return by way of Cambridge Bay Post."[3]

The men glimpsed a mirage to the west of Dishwater Point and took it to be a good omen for the next day's journey. This sight appeared to be the reflection of the straits they needed to cross and also of what appeared to be Bathurst Inlet. Both early Arctic expedition members and modern-day Northern explorers write about the refraction of the Arctic light and how tricks can be played on the eyes. Tales have been told of icebergs floating in the sky and great phantom ice-covered mountain ranges looming out of the Arctic Ocean. However, the light refraction on the snow, which created the mirage, gave the men hope for the anticipated trip.

Thompson decided to shave for the occasion, and Pearce assisted with scissors. Once shaved, Thompson no longer resembled the old feudal lord. The rest of the men busied themselves getting the food ready for travel. Caribou steaks were cut and an inventory was taken of the remaining "bush fare." They still had three tins of beef, the chocolate bars, thirty Oxo cubes, a slab of bacon, eight hard-tack biscuits, and a very small amount of cocoa. The Inuit added tea, coffee, and the primus stove for the walk out.

Before the last light, the group lined up for a farewell photo. This would be a fitful night's sleep. Their minds were jumping, restless with anticipation and hopeful that nothing more would delay their trek to the post at Cambridge Bay. Their group strength was bound by both determination and their desire to reach the outside world. They would need it for the demanding journey.

Courtesy of Daryl Goodwin.

The Dominion Explorers and their Inuit guides stand for a formal photo just prior to beginning the trek to Cambridge Bay. The Inuit had done their best to ensure each member of the group were as warmly dressed as possible and had even made "hats" out of seagull skin to keep heads warm.

Andy prepared his report for WCA: "All machines were hauled ashore up well-oiled planks for a Slipway. 'A.R.K' the Northern Arial Mineral Exploration machine was nearest the water, tail outwards. To all appearances especially as the lake had already a thin skin of ice, all machines were perfectly safe and tied down…."

At Baker Lake, the men readied the planes for ski landings. The northwest shore of the lake was open water when they arrived, but the temperature was dropping. The changeover from floats to skis was exhausting. It took several men to remove and lift the float and the undercarriage. Once this was done, an undercarriage equipped with a ski was attached on each side. The changeover was time-consuming, with only one plane being done at a time.

Ice that formed on the lake during the night still broke up frequently during the days, causing some concern. Despite this, all seemed to be going well, but that was about to change. Cruickshank's sixth sense was nudging him.

The air engineers adjust the skis on Roy Brown's 'SO. These skis were manufactured by the Elliot Brothers of Sioux Lookout, Ontario, and were built to withstand the harsh landings in the frozen North.

Provincial Archives of Manitoba, Canadian Air Lines Collection #587.

Early in the evening on the 17th, the men were in the Révillon Frères Trading Post at Baker Lake, playing poker with the RCMP constable and Dr. Bruce. Andy Cruickshank felt he needed some fresh air, so he folded his cards and walked out to the beach. He sat on the shoreline writing a poem to Esmé. It was their second wedding anniversary. He called Esmé his "star" and in his poem wrote about how he missed her. As he wrote, the wind began to pick up and the premonition intensified. He walked over to the planes to make sure they were tied securely and hoped that his sense of foreboding was misplaced.

Tonight would be a night to remember.

During the changeover from floats to skis, the five planes had been squeezed into a very tight space on the beach outside the trading post. Three could have fit there comfortably. Once the wind started to blow, Cruickshank knew they were in for more trouble. He braced himself and waited. Just after midnight the uncontrollable wrath of nature unleashed its power.

"The beach is collapsing!" His call for help pierced the night, bringing the men out of the post. In his report to Western Canada Airlines, Cruickshank recorded: "We had a terrible storm from the East, which sprayed "A.R.K." ['RK] forming ice on the tail plane elevators and rudder, gradually weighing the tail down. The force of the storm then threw tremendous waves bearing large pieces of ice far up on the shore smashing the elevators and rudders. All hands worked nearly all night hauling her further ashore."

Besieged by Arctic blasts, freezing rain, and darkness, the men attempted the near impossible — to turn each aircraft around, facing outward, to protect the more fragile tail assemblies. As they laboured, the wind broke the thin ice up into a sharp, churning mass, cracking and shifting under their feet and slicing their legs. The spray slammed into the tail of Vance's 'RK, freezing on contact, its weight pulling the tail and rudders down and destroying the tail assembly. Having been the most exposed, and the one that had not been changed to skis, it bore the brunt of nature's assault.

In the morning light, the men stood at the edge of Baker Lake. They were exhausted, soaking wet, cold, and disheartened — they had not been able to save the severely damaged 'RK. It looked like a wounded bird, with its tail and rudders broken and its wings poised at odd angles. T.W. Siers, the maintenance manager for Western Canada Airways, described the event in his report: "In the dark the machine was turned 180 degrees in so confined a space that the task seemed utterly impossible when seen in daylight."[4]

Knowing there was no possibility of fixing the damaged plane without parts and tools, the men continued to prepare the remaining four planes to fly out to Bathurst Inlet. The Fokkers 'SQ and 'SO had been changed over from floats to skis without problem, but the Fairchild had both main shock absorber struts missing, and the tail ski and tailskid had not been sent. Nevertheless, the mechanics managed to fashion struts from a radio mast.

Tommy Siers documented the work done by the mechanics during the wait at Baker Lake: "The mast was made of 3" galvanized pipe. The ends were heated and flattened, then a piece of keel strip was taken from an old motor boat and driven into the flattened ends and bolted into place and holes drilled for attaching to the machine."[5] Since the mechanics couldn't find any large bolts, they used the standard hardware bolts, most likely made from softer steel. It was the only choice they had, but one that would present a grave problem in the future. Siers used an ordinary garden shovel for the tailskid, and they continued to do their best with what they had at hand, which proved to be remarkable in retrospect.

It wasn't all work, however. The men did take time to play a few rounds of darts during some well-deserved down time. Nadin fashioned a dartboard out of a large tree trunk. He cut a two-inch piece off the end of the trunk, about the right size for a board, and with soft wire sectioned off the dartboard and numbered the sections. He then crafted darts using round pieces of wood, fitted with salvaged gramophone needles. Nadin then found a way to make feathers out of paper. Such pastimes provided a welcome distraction from the problems they were facing.[6]

While the mechanics were working on the aircraft, Cruickshank and the other pilots continued hauling gas on Dominion Explorer dogsleds to a small lake about one mile away, where the ice had formed a good, solid base. This ice would allow the planes to take off with lighter loads from Baker, land on the solid surface of the smaller lake, and then load the planes for their flight to Bathurst. But they still needed a takeoff runway to accommodate ski planes.

Finding a suitable place for this runway was another challenge. Cruickshank measured and marked off an area behind the Révillon Frères Trading Post. The area was littered with small stones, which could create a hazard for the skis, so the men worked for hours with pickaxes and shovels to make a runway passable for the aircraft. Although he wasn't sure that it would even be used, Cruickshank wanted the men to be active and have something to do in light of the fact that freeze-up had not yet taken place. A purpose-driven

Karram Family Collection.

Dog teams like Cruickshank's were the primary means of transporting goods in the Far North. Travel by dog team is anything but easy, and no matter how well-trained the team is the musher can be subjected to "decisions" made by the dogs and be tossed or taken for quite the ride.

man, Cruickshank knew the importance of keeping busy. His goal was to keep the men occupied both mentally and physically to prevent any further loss of morale.

As anticipated, despite the hard work and clearing, the makeshift runway strip remained unsuitable for takeoff. The temperature had been dropping during the day and the broken ice that had been driven in towards the shore during the storm on the 17th, once frozen solid, again produced a very rugged but thick surface on which to take off and land. Cruickshank decided to try a second runway on the shore of Baker Lake, so once again all hands then went to work with ice picks, shovels, and axes. Once this was complete, the search team was then able to taxi the planes over to where the gas had been cached. Cruikshank's diary entry, dated October 21, 1929, Baker Lake, noted: "Got SO over today and gassed up all machines. Test flew SQ. Running quite reasonable. SL brought over, [but] rudder does not seem to be properly adjusted. Expect to leave for Bathurst tomorrow. All machines tested."

Cruikshank used the wireless to notify Western Canada Airways of their imminent departure for Bathurst Inlet. On October 17, 1929, *The Northern Miner* reported on the actions of the rescuers, whom they labelled "Canada's Wild Geese." In the article, these men were portrayed as engaging in work that called for nerve, expertise, and courage. Canada was enthralled with the accounts of the group of Canadian men who were part of an effort that was unique in the world, pilots who had to rely on their skills and resourcefulness, rather than solely on their equipment.

The four remaining planes — the Fokkers 'SQ, 'SO, and 'SL, and the Fairchild 'CZ — were now ready to fly to the Arctic coast. Cruickshank was not happy about leaving Vance and Blasdale at Baker Lake, but until parts arrived for the damaged plane, they would continue to work on 'RK. It was some consolation to know that they would have both company and warm shelter with the other men living at the trading post. The searchers packed up their kits, loaded the four planes, and prepared to head northwards towards Bathurst.

Meanwhile, October 21 at Dishwater Point began with dashed hopes. The departure date the Domex men had awaited for weeks had finally arrived, only to be delayed yet again. The thought of staying on in the collapsing sod house was more than they could bear. Baker decided a bribe might just be what was needed to get the Inuit to leave Dishwater Point. He asked Pearce to get the rifles and ammunition, and presented them to the Inuit.

From the time of the arrival of the Europeans in the North, guns were a sought-after possession for the Inuit. The caribou migrations had been changing and game was not as plentiful as it had been, causing the Inuit to begin to change their subsistence way of life.[7] The relentless hunt for game such as caribou, muskox, fox, and Arctic hare, more easily killed with guns, made gun ownership very desirable. In fact, the Arctic fox was the standard of value for trade, and twenty Arctic fox skins were worth one rifle. Trading skins for items such as flour was becoming increasingly popular, and hunting with a gun enabled the Inuit to more easily provide for his family.[8] An Inuit with a rifle was a hunter in the new world.

Courtesy of Daryl Goodwin.

Harnessing the dogs and loading last minute provisions on the sleds. The rifle, given to the Inuit, is propped up against an igloo.

These gifts had the impact that Major Baker was hoping for, and by 8:00 a.m. the men had packed up and were ready to go on their trek to Cambridge Bay. Three dog teams, each with an Inuit guide and his wife, took charge of the Domex men. The howling excited dogs settled down once their masters called them to work. Fifty-nine days after the Dominion Explorers had taken off from Winnipeg on their journey in search of minerals, their efforts were now focused on a journey that they hoped would bring them home. The going would be anything but easy.

October 21, 1929
Richard Pearce's Diary, en route to Cambridge Bay

We are about 25 miles from the old mud shack, camped opposite the end of Melbourne Island. We found out that dog-team travelling is not like it appears in the movies, with speeding dogs carrying mushers along. The real stuff is largely hard work, real hard going when the snow is a little soft ... The boys are feeling muscles they never knew they had and the Colonel had to lean on me for a few minutes tonight to get rid of a cramp in the leg. The Eskimos built snow igloos and put them up in no time. While the temperature in them must be kept below freezing, they are quite comfortable ... This will have to be all for tonight as I am too tired to write more.

The group, though exhausted, was pleased with the distance travelled. Dashing behind the dog teams, over a surface that was anything but even, left them completely worn out, bruised, and feeling unmercifully battered. The dwindling Arctic light made it difficult to discern the ridges made by the blowing snow, and the men stumbled and fell throughout the day. Pearce commented,

"Three weeks ago we could not have done it. However, we are doing the very thing we have wanted to do for weeks, and a little tired feeling is not likely to stop us on our way to the post."[9] All continued to be busy until the igloos were constructed and the dogs had been tended.

The building of an igloo is a remarkable feat. The very idea seems strange in itself, as the materials used to protect from the storms and cold are the same materials made by freezing temperatures and driving snow. Yet the Inuit had been building igloos for shelter since their life was established in the land of snow and ice, and they went about their task efficiently and quickly. The igloo is built in a spiral, out of 24x4x14-inch blocks, each weighing about thirty pounds. Not any type of snow will do. The blocks must be cut out of a drift that is firm enough to be handled by the builder, then placed in a spiral manner, each block having two weight-bearing edges. A snow knife, with a very long and extremely sharp blade, is the only tool needed.[10] The blocks are cut vertically into the drift, and the depression created by the removal of the blocks will be the main room of the igloo, giving the family inside enough headroom to stand. Each block is fitted closely and made secure with a very sharp "pat." The walls rise at an astonishing rate and remain secure regardless of the slope, because of the dense consistency of the snow. The flat-lying blocks forming the top require extra attention and shaping, and the key block at the very top is fitted snugly to close the igloo. If the igloo is not being built just for the night, the builder may use a clear piece of ice for a window.[11]

Once the igloo was finished, the Domex men removed all traces of snow from their clothing before entering the dwelling. This task was achieved by beating the parkas with a stick. Inside their soundproof and insulated igloos they chatted about the day's accomplishment while the evening meal was being prepared. The foremost part of the igloo was used for cooking; the Coleman stove was lit and the food was pooled. Trout, dried salmon, a little bacon, and "other odds and ends" added together made a fine, hearty, and enjoyable meal. Once the evening meal was finished and cleaned up, it was time to settle in for a well-deserved rest.

The back of the igloos consisted of a ledge built out of snow blocks. This ledge was the sleeping platform for the men. Since cold air falls, the ledge kept the sleeping bodies at a warmer elevation. The Inuit laid out willow mats and skins to cover the snow ledge, and this became the beds on which the bone-weary bodies slept, their heads toward the centre of the igloo, again to keep a distance from the frozen igloo walls.

Just before they went to sleep, a *kovik* was passed around. This strange implement, the Inuit version of a chamber pot, was made out of a muskox horn and resembling a dipper-like utensil. It was used by one after the other, and the contents were dumped in front of the sleeping bench, where they disappeared into the snow.[12] A seal lamp was left burning during the night, which cast dancing shadows on the icy walls and produced a sense of comfort. The trek was calculated to take three days and two nights.

Both the Domex men and the searchers flying under Cruickshank's direction had made their moves. Both their efforts would be thwarted.

FIVE

Crash of G-CASQ

October 22, 1929
Richard Pearce's Diary, en route to Cambridge Bay

Our igloo caved in this morning with the warmer weather and we had to stay in bed while the Eskimos repaired it. There was snow everywhere, but it was all carefully cleaned up … We started off at 9:45 and had good going for only a few miles, after which it got soft. It did not take long for the dogs to play out and we stopped at four, after covering only eight or ten miles. We went up a high hill and saw open water in the straits. We will have to stay where we are until the weather becomes colder and a crust forms on the snow … The Eskimos tell us we would be able to make the post from here in one day, and we hope to start again in the morning. We are tired, but anxious to move to the post.

The weary travellers again were at the mercy of the weather. They were a desperate group that had felt the adrenaline rush when they left Dishwater Point, but now their hopes melted just as quickly as the ice. October 23 dawned warmer than the previous day. The Eskimos told the Domex men to remain in bed, which they heartily agreed to do. One of the igloos caved in for the second time in two days, creating the necessity to build another. Their coal oil, which was used for cooking the food, was running out and the prospect of eating raw, cold food again was a dismal thought. Things were not looking good for the trek to Cambridge Bay.

To their delight, the 24th was colder and the Domex men and the Inuit were on the move once again. This day, however, turned out to be a difficult one. The group hit upon great walls of ice, several feet in height, which made progress almost impossible. Soon, the dogs were completely exhausted, and the men had to haul the sleds over the rough terrain. Their clothing became soaked with sweat, which froze once they stopped moving. Despite the icy blasts buffeting the exhausted group, they managed to cover twenty-five miles. After darkness fell, the Inuit constructed igloos

Courtesy of Daryl Goodwin.

The Dominion Explorers take a well-deserved pause during the long journey to Cambridge Bay. An Inuit child rests on top of the komatic, *a sled used to transport goods in the North.*

again, a feat in itself for the speed and precision with which they completed the task, and they settled in for the night in relative comfort. Tea helped wash down the meager rations of fish both raw and boiled. The colonel, however, only ate a piece of chocolate the size of a quarter. Dinner was eaten in bed, to offset the chill of wet clothing. They also took their boots to bed with them, in an attempt to dry them out.

Morale perked up when they awoke to a very cold day. It was a day of much-needed loafing to recuperate and to gain strength for the next part of the journey. Some of the members climbed a snowdrift to survey the crossing and were delighted to see a frozen strait. Jack brought out some tobacco, which the men agreed was the absolute worst ever. As they discussed their situation they reflected that their Inuit caretakers certainly had their best interests at heart when they refused to attempt an earlier crossing, as the outcome could only have been a disaster. The subject of a search was also not far from their minds, and the men held out hope that rescue planes would be coming soon to meet them at Cambridge Bay. Weather, however, was not being kind to the search teams either.

———

On October 22, the men at Baker Lake made final preparations for the trip north to Bathurst Inlet. They had agreed that if the waters were still open at Bathurst, they would attempt a landing at Burnside River at a Domex prospecting camp established the previous summer. If waters were still open at Burnside River, they would find some small frozen lake nearby to land on and set up a base until the river was frozen. The flight would be a risky one, as they would be flying with skis, sooner than normal judgment would permit, over both open waters and thinly ice-covered lakes. An emergency landing could be hazardous, not only for the pilot and crew, but also for the other fliers who would come to their aid.

Courtesy of Western Canada Aviation Museum.

The air fleet, with extra cans of gas, is ready for its flight to Bathurst Inlet.

The throb of the engines shattered the Arctic stillness as Cruickshank, Spence, Hollick-Kenyon, and Brown started their engines. Running an airplane in the Arctic deep freeze was truly an art form, particularly the warm-up. The frigid temperatures could easily cause the metal on the planes to become brittle, making it imperative to give each plane sufficient time to warm up. Despite modern technological innovations, this problem has not yet been completely solved. Even now, if the temperature of the engine is insufficient, cracked cylinders, oil starvation, and ruptured seals can occur. The last thing any of the searchers needed was another aircraft out of commission.

Once all the pilots had checked their planes, Cruickshank, Hollick-Kenyon, and Brown took to the air safely, but Bill Spence was not so lucky. As he taxied, he bounced heavily on a frozen drift, and lost control of his plane, smashing a tail ski.

Cruickshank banked his plane and looked down to make sure all the aircraft had safely taken flight and immediately saw that Spence had hit trouble. The planned flight came to an abrupt end.

The pilots landed their three aircraft and promptly tied them down at the edge of the shore. It was good fortune that spare parts could be pulled from Vance's plane, and all hands set to work, removing a skid and tail ski from 'RK. They hoped that the replacement parts would remain stable for the next landing.

Cruickshank noted in his diary that the engineers also created some parts to make the necessary repairs to 'CZ. The work on Spence's plane halted the flight for the remainder of the day, a source of frustration for the searchers. They had no choice but to but spend another night at the Baker Lake base.

A dense fog hugged the ground for the next two days, once more delaying the flight to Bathurst. Often mist or fog could change to heavy, wet snow, which would not only obscure the ground but block visibility for the pilots during flight and landing. This type of snow pattern was often low and drifted erratically with the variable winds.[1] There was nothing they could do but wait.

———

Finally, on October 25 the weather permitted the journey northward to Bathurst. After circling the post, the four pilots set their course and climbed to five thousand feet in formation. Flying was good for some time, but they soon sighted a swirling great cloud field ahead, so each one dropped to one thousand feet, hoping they would be able to fly under the dense cover.[2] Within minutes there was zero visibility:

> October 25, 1929
> Andy Cruickshank's Diary, Baker Lake to Burnside
>
> During our flight to Bathurst we ran into bad fog conditions. At times our machines were not in sight of each other although only a few yards apart. I strongly recommend that under no

circumstances should aircraft try to fly through fog in formation, and only under exceptional circumstances should any pilot fly anywhere in the Barrens unless the sun is visible ... Spence flying on my left very close, disappeared in dense cloud. Last I saw of his machine was Spence cutting across my bow at about 20 yards ahead climbing fast. I dived to miss him and landed at once on a nearby lake. Took off later to look for other machines but couldn't see more than 200 yards. Decided to wait till morning....

Once 'SQ had landed, Cruickshank and his crew went hunting. Semple was certain he could bring in some dinner, and although they saw no game, caribou and fox tracks were plentiful. Even though the hunt was unsuccessful, the men still enjoyed their bush rations, and, after this makeshift dinner, climbed into their eiderdowns and settled down for a night on the ice.

Cruickshank knew from his experience in the Yukon that camping on the ice, bizarre as it may sound, was indeed warmer than camping on terra firma. The water temperature below the layer of ice was about -1.1°C, whereas on land, the temperature of the ground could be as cold as in the -40s. Sleep was another matter. Because of the cold temperatures under the sleeping rolls, the men's body temperature would drop during the night, causing fits of shivering — a natural reflex in response to the temperature change. The reflex triggers the shaking of muscle groups around vital organs and creates warmth by expending energy, with heat being the by-product of the increased muscular activity. Shivering, of course, would also waken the outdoor sleeper. Once the body regulated its internal environment and caused his body temperature to rise, he would then, if lucky, go back to sleep only to be awakened again about two hours later when the core body temperatures had dropped once more to the point that causes the shivering. This sleep disruption went on all night long.

On October 26, Alf Walker and the others began the routine to get 'SQ ready for flight, a task made more challenging by the weather. In the Arctic freeze-up, the morning temperature was well below zero, and often the engineer would sleep with his flashlight to prevent the batteries from freezing. At this time of year every air engineer had to ready the plane for flight in darkness. Preparations took time and were anything but simple.

The air engineer's first job was to cut kindling and make a fire near the airplane. A tarp (the engine tent), which had been thrown over the plane's engine the previous night, provided a makeshift hangar. He would then light two heating torches, making sure a fire extinguisher was at hand, and begin the arduous and dangerous task of heating both the engine and the engine oil. Though fumes from the torches would quickly fill the space and his lungs, he had to keep alert and watchful in case an unseen drop of fuel should cause a fire, which within minutes could transform the plane into an inferno. Once the oil had been heated over the fire and the engine warmed, the engineer removed the torches and would quickly pour the oil into the tanks, pull off the canvas "hangar," hand crank the engine, and, with fingers crossed, hope to hear the staccato roar of the engine. Next he would wait for the engine and oil to reach temperatures warm enough to permit flight. If the engine did not come to life, the oil would need to be drained quickly and the process started all over again.[3]

Prior to takeoff, Walker also needed to inspect the plane for any damage or ice on the wings. Icing could easily spell disaster because ice formation on the edge of the wings hampers the lift of the aircraft and can result in a crash. The skis also needed special attention, as did an appropriate runway. A smashed ski would be critical since there were no spare parts to be had on this remote, unnamed lake. Luckily for Walker, both Semple and Cruickshank were also certified air engineers, and they helped him ready the craft for takeoff. Once the airworthiness was approved, they stowed their gear, climbed aboard, and taxied on the icy surface, polishing the frost from the bottom of the skis. Then Cruickshank opened the throttle and put the nose of the plane in the air. It did not seem to worry these men, or at least they did not express concern that they were flying solo, without assurance or help from any other plane or crew, if help was needed.

Within minutes Cruickshank spotted Brown, Hollick-Kenyon, and Spence just ahead. As it happened, the other three pilots had landed on a frozen lake not far from where Cruickshank and his crew had spent the night. Cruickshank increased his speed and took his place in the formation. For the next few hours the four pilots and their crew searched along the route to Bathurst Inlet.

> October 26, 1929
> Andy Cruickshank's Diary, somewhere above the Arctic Circle
>
> The country was absolutely barren, not a living creature was seen during the entire trip. The terrain was of a rolling rocky nature with thousands of lakes, some of immense size. Twenty or so miles before reaching Bathurst Inlet the terrain changed and became a series of mountains of ragged rock of approximately one thousand to fifteen hundred feet in elevation.

When the pilots reached Bathurst they found only open water, making it impossible to land with ski-equipped planes. Flying south as planned, they located the very small Domex camp at Burnside River where they hoped that the ice would be strong enough to support the landings of four fully loaded planes.

———

Ice continued to be the issue both for the rescue teams and for the Domex men and their guides.

October 25, 1929
Richard Pearce's Diary, Kent Peninsula

Another day of blasted hopes. We got up at five — or at least the alarm went off then — and had our breakfast of half slice of bacon and a little piece of fish. We got away in good time and were making nice headway over rough hummocks of ice when we bumped into open water. It was a real blow. Our course was switched and we ran alongside the water half a mile or so, and found that tide and wind had united to make a break 100 yards or so wide between us and Cambridge Bay.

The men were devastated. Nearly a quarter of the way across the strait, they had no choice but to turn back to where they had begun their day. Since the igloos had deteriorated in the intervening hours, the Inuit did repairs and rebuilt another large structure. All were dismayed by their slow progress and the setback.

The next day dawned warmer and the Inuit, who had thus far been the most accurate weather predictors, said more warm weather was on the way. One would think that the far reaches of the Arctic Circle would be covered in ice, yet during the latter weeks of October 1929, cold temperatures had given way to a warm spell that had melted the ice in the strait.

The group was down to very sparse rations. The food consisted of whitefish and herring, which just happened to be the food brought for the dogs. None of the men wanted to cheat the dogs, who had been working so hard, but there was no option. Pearce commented, "There is a lot better food in the world, but it is a question of root, hog, or die, and life is sweet."[4] The Inuit decided the only option was to send Charlie and Jimmie back to Dease Point for supplies.

When the "three-day" trek to Cambridge Bay began, they had packed enough food for seven days. Seven days had now passed, but still the group was nowhere near the Hudson's Bay Post at Cambridge Bay. Charlie and Jimmie anticipated a two-day return journey and set off with a dog team of eleven to bring back more dog food and the food the Domex men had left in their planes for trophies. They had caught some fine trout while at Dishwater Point, which they intended to mount for the colonel and Pearce when they returned to Winnipeg. There were ground squirrels as well, to be taken to a taxidermist upon arrival home. Food for survival, however, was far more essential than a scrap of fur or a trout mounted on a wall!

October 28, 1929
Richard Pearce's Diary, Kent Peninsula

As the Eskimos prophesied, it is another warm day. The other igloo fell in, and ours shows signs of following suit. Charlie and Jimmie should be back either tomorrow or the next day and we are hoping to have a good feed before starting for Cambridge. The morale of the occupants of the other igloo is not so high today. The caving in of the igloo is perhaps responsible. It is now seven weeks since we landed at Dease Point. It seems more like seven years … The ice conditions in the straits is not very satisfactory today. A wind came up and big leads show close to shore. We had three meals of dog feed today, and it remains to be seen how it is going to affect the Colonel and me. Some of the other boys have had spells of sickness.

Living on such scant rations weakened the group both physically and mentally. The strain they were under was almost unbearable. Stomachs were reacting violently to what was being consumed as food, and there was not a thing they could do about it. Just when they thought things couldn't get worse, one igloo caved in and the second was showing signs of doing the same. Both food and shelter were no longer sources of comfort and solace, but of frustration and trepidation.

Major Baker remarked that he could do without food, but being without tobacco was more than he could stand. The colonel and Pearce took pity on him, and between the two of them emptied their pockets and scraped up enough tobacco together to make one cigarette, which they rolled in toilet paper. A very grateful Baker savoured that single cigarette, making it last as long as he could.

A wind was blowing, much to the horror of the group who were acutely aware that a very thin layer of ice was all that stood between them and drowning. This wind continued to increase the leads (expanses of seawater opened when the ice began to fracture) in the strait, making the crossing impossible. A small crack in the ice could expand to a broad gap of icy water within minutes, which could result in their being stranded on a small ice floe. They estimated that there were about thirty-eight miles to go to Cambridge Bay, but it may as well have been the same distance as to the moon, because, unless the waters froze, they were trapped.

———

Only two hundred miles away, the rescue pilots were circling the waters at Burnside River. From the air, the ice appeared to be suitable for a ski landing. Spence was the first to touch down. To his relief, the ice held. Brown followed suit, landing in Spence's tracks. Both planes taxied further down the ice before cutting their engines. Cruickshank was third to land, but as he touched down, the ice, degraded by the rough landings of 'CZ and 'SO and now rubbery, gave way under his skis. 'SQ, with Cruickshank, Walker, and Semple aboard, plunged into the icy depths of Burnside River.

Courtesy of Western Canada Aviation Museum.

Cruickshank and crew felt the rotten ice give way under their fully-loaded plane, and they plunged, nose-first, into the frigid waters of the Burnside River.

The propeller and engine hit full force into the ice with a deafening crash. Frigid water and chunks of ice rushed into the cockpit through the ripped fuselage and open cracks and seams in the aluminum cowling. Hollick-Kenyon, still airborne, watched in horror as 'SQ's cockpit sank with her crew still on board. Spence and Brown saw the crash and had killed the engines on their planes, but since a ski plane has no brakes, they had to wait for the drag friction of the ice to slow their planes to a complete stop. Pushing open the side doors, the men clambered out of 'CZ and 'SO and raced towards the wreckage.

Unable to get to 'SQ because of the broken ice surrounding the plane, they could only stand powerlessly and watch for signs of life.

| Six |

Peril on Ice

October 27, 1929
Andy Cruickshank's Diary, Burnside River

Ice broke and ship [plane] sank immediately ... Engine
completely submerged, cabin and cockpit full of ice and water.

From the air the scene below looked horrific. Hollick-Kenyon needed
a safe place to land his plane, but he could not shake the image of
the submerged 'SQ. Not knowing whether Andy Cruickshank, Alf
Walker, and Pat Semple had survived, he forced his pilot's training
to override his fears and flew on without conscious thought. He
continued further on down Burnside River until he spotted an open
area. He lined up his landing path and descended. Pilot and crew held

their breath as the skis touched down. Thankfully, the ice held and 'SL and crew landed safely. After securing the aircraft, the adrenaline-charged men dashed back, barely able to breathe, to the scene of the crash. It would be the longest two-and-a-half miles they had ever run, but also perhaps the fastest, at least on that frigid terrain.

At the crash site the men from the Burnside post and the pilots and crews of the other planes watched helplessly. The impact of the crash had broken the ice into great chunks, and the seawater was seeping up among them, making it impossible to reach 'SQ. Time stood still.

All were greatly relieved when Cruickshank threw open the overhead hatch above the pilot's cockpit, and three very wet, cold, and shaken men emerged from the wreckage. With freezing fingers, the badly shaken pilot and crew grappled hand over hand along the twenty-five foot length of a wing until their feet touched stable ice. As the onlookers gathered round, Cruickshank shook off offers of help and expressions of concern, commenting only that as soon as his skis had touched down he knew he was in trouble. The eroding force of the currents, combined with the powerful impacts of 'CZ and 'SO, had destabilized the ice beneath the skis of 'SQ. Taxiing along the same tracks as Brown and Spence weakened the surface even more, but there was not a thing he could do to forestall the inevitable — the ice simply gave way under the weight of his fully loaded plane, and the aircraft sank into the icy water of the Burnside River.[1]

The engine and cockpit were completely submerged and filled with ice and salt water, while the wings rested on the surface of the broken ice. Some windows of the aircraft had been cracked (thankfully, not the overhead hatch) and there was a very large tear in the fuselage. The propeller tips were bent, the carburetor and magnetos were soaked, and the instruments and cylinders were full of water. (Magnetos are the electrical generators that provide the current to the spark plugs in an internal combustion engine.) The rescue team was now reduced from the five original search planes to three. This was a huge blow, as it meant that the area they could

After Cruickshank, Semple, and Walker climb out of the overhead hatch and gather their wits about them, they discuss their options.

cover in a day of searching was almost halved, effectively doubling the time needed to accomplish their mission. The possibility of success was becoming increasingly remote.

———

The Domex men were struggling on:

October 29, 1929
Richard Pearce's Diary, 39 miles from Cambridge
Bay

This is our fifth day here and by the look of things it will not be the last. A stiff wind threatens to break up the ice floes between here and Cambridge. In the afternoon the barometer dropped and there is every reason to believe the storm we are having will become worse. The boys are feeling glummer than they have for some time and some have expressed the wish that we had not left the mud shack with its stove at Dease Point. Of course, the toughest part of it all is the admission from the Eskimos that we probably could have crossed the straits the day after we landed. However, here we are and here we'll stay a while … Our supper tonight was raw fish. It is hard going, but down it went.

Life was anything but easy on this harsh and treacherous portion of the Arctic coast. October 30 dawned colder, with the wind changing direction. A delicate pink light rinsed the landscape, creating an eerie, luminescent glow, but there was nothing delicate about the fierce cold that bullied them unmercifully. The wind cut into their lungs like a knife and their nasal passages crackled and bled. Frostbite was a major concern. Lacking mirrors, the men frequently inspected one another for telltale patches of white on their faces.

The Domex men had learned to live by the terms demanded by the Arctic, and they stayed inside their igloos waiting for conditions to change. Knowing that he needed food in order to generate body heat, Pearce was enticed to eat a little seal blubber for breakfast that day, something he wrote he would never do again. There was very little food left, and unless Charlie and Jimmie arrived back before nightfall, both the dogs and the humans would be completely out of sustenance. In what was possibly hunger-induced imaginings, a very peculiar thought came into Pearce's head. What if the residents at Cambridge Bay might not take the Domex men in because they smelled of seal oil? Where would they go then?

As well as disordered thinking, emotional fragility was another effect of chronic hunger. Powerless and frustrated, the men could do nothing to change nature's moods. Smouldering anger and frustration finally erupted. Rumblings of mutiny surfaced, and some of the expedition members gave notice to Major Baker that they could not stand the waiting anymore and they would be attempting to cross the strait in the morning, with or without the help of the Inuit. This would be the first act of open rebellion, and one that was bound to fail. Navigating the treacherous pressure ridges, ice hummocks, and the possible deadly channels of open water without the Inuit could only spell disaster. MacAlpine was acutely aware of this and the necessity to follow the Inuit decisions, yet he was equally aware that he was losing control. He knew a small mistake in judgment in this remote region of the earth could easily mean death, but for that matter, even good decisions would not guarantee survival. They would need luck as well as the Inuit skill for their trek through the labyrinth of the Arctic channels towards Cambridge Bay.

October 30, 1929
Richard Pearce's Diary, Peechuk Point

Major Baker, while agreeing to the probability of good ice across the straits, told them they could do what they chose, but that in his opinion a change in the wind might again cause the ice to break and form floes and the attempt should not be made without food (which we did not possess) as they might be caught on an ice floe for several days. If they went, they did so on their own responsibility and directly against the Colonel's expressed wishes of playing safety first. We were with the Eskimos who knew ice conditions and would take us over at the first safe opportunity. Furthermore, the party was not to cross without being accompanied by the Eskimos. Major Baker discussed the situation with the Colonel and it was agreed that if Charlie did not return tomorrow and Major Baker could persuade one of the Eskimos to go that he would do so in order to get possible communication by wireless out from Cambridge Bay. This is the saddest entry I have made in my diary, but I feel it is a case of empty stomach and low morale. We have named this place Peechuk Point because the Eskimos use "Peechuk" for all gone, and we are pretty well out of food.

It is remarkable how much disappointment, despair and hopelessness one can stand, and yet somehow find the will to carry on. Hopelessness can and, in both the Dominion Explorers and searchers cases, did lead to both resourcefulness and resilience beyond expectation.

Tommy Siers looked at the submerged 'SQ and said, "The only way we are getting this plane back to Winnipeg is to fly it there, so let's get to work."[2] As head mechanic, only Siers could make this decision, and it would prove to be pivotal in the lives of all the men.

The salvage operation began. The aircraft was supported on the ice by the undersurface of the wings, and the skis had touched bottom in the shallow water, making the plane somewhat stable. It was imperative that 'SQ be removed from the ice and salt water in the best condition possible, but with the frigid temperatures the ice was beginning to form where the plane had broken through. Lying on their stomachs and using their bare hands, the men passed a rope into the freezing water and fastened it around the crankshaft of the engine, behind the propeller hub. This was just the beginning in what came to be the most extensive salvage operation in the history of Western Canada Airways.[3]

The following morning, October 28, while the mechanics, dubbed "the black gang," worked in the freezing temperatures, the pilots in 'SO and 'CZ began to search the Arctic coast. Having covered the area from Baker Lake to Bathurst and Burnside River, Cruickshank decided that the next area to search would be Ellice River and the surrounding coast. Since the cache had been emptied at Beverly Lake and the Dominion Explorers had never arrived at Bathurst Inlet, he reasoned that the expedition had most likely flown off course due to the winds, bad weather, and inaccurate compass readings because of the magnetic North Pole.

The men discussed possible scenarios. Cruickshank felt that the planes could have run out of gas and likely landed somewhere on the coast. Refusing to entertain the possibility of both planes going down, he therefore surmised that fuel would have been the problem. He only hoped that they had been able to survive for the past seven weeks. Landing near an Inuit camp would mean the best chance of survival, and since there were gathering points of the Inuit at both the mouth of the Ellice River and Dease Point, these would be the next areas in which to perform the search.[4]

Once airborne, the planes headed eastward following the Ellice River then north toward the Arctic coast along the Kent Peninsula. In such a massive area of the Northwest Territories, it might seem amazing that Cruickshank had sent the search planes right over the area where the downed Domex party had been stranded for the past seven weeks. At the same time, it is another indication of his intimate knowledge of the region.

Unfortunately, neither the pilots nor crews of 'SO and 'CZ saw the tiny camp at Dease Point, but they must have been quite close because later in Pearce's diary he mentions the Inuit hearing planes flying overhead. The area was encrusted with a layer of snow covering the planes, sod house, and the surrounding shattered rock. Inuit staying at Dease Point had been asked to keep the wings of the planes clean, but unfortunately this had not been done. The reality was that this was a challenging area in which to search, and one that was mostly unmapped. All that could be seen from above was a rippling expanse of white, the lakes indistinguishable from land. Visibility was exceptionally poor, but Brown and Spence, with their crews, kept flying.

The Bathurst Mountains were spattered with patches of exposed black rock, and eyes strained at each dark object that could be mistaken for a group of men. Time and time again they thought they had spotted a downed aircraft or survivors, but when flying in for a closer look realized bleakly that they had been fooled by the uneven teeth of the rocky outcrops. Having had no luck, 'SO and 'CZ crews returned via the southern neck of the Kent Peninsula, hugging the western coast of Bathurst Inlet to the base at Burnside River.

Hollick-Kenyon flew sixty miles to Bathurst Inlet to send messages to Winnipeg, where Western Canada Airways had their head office, and to Dominion Explorers in Toronto. Both were anxiously waiting for news of the search operation. With Vance's plane being a write-off until parts could be obtained, and now 'SQ in questionable shape, the bad news had to be told. Up until now, the searchers had been forging ahead with their own plans, a policy agreeable to both WCA and Dominion Explorers, yet, when possible, information of the actions being taken needed to be sent to Winnipeg and Toronto through the wireless. After checking on the condition of the ice and finding open water he dropped messages to be picked up by the people at the Hudson's Bay Post. 'SL then made a search along the coast, again not seeing any sign of the missing men or their planes.

For the next two days, poor weather kept the search crew grounded, so the men put all their efforts into the salvage operation of Cruickshank's 'SQ, now deemed "the old crock." Siers reported:

> A piece of timber 8"x8"x18' was rigged up as a gin pole in front of the engine, its base resting on the ocean bed. Two double blocks were used and the machine gradually came up through the ice but it was found that the weight of the machine sank the gin pole into the mud. To overcome this a 3"x6"x10' piece of timber was lashed and nailed to the 8"x8" and the hitch changed from the 8"x8" to the 3"x6". This change allowed the machine to be lifted clear of the water and ice. There was a slight but uneven tide. This in itself was a source of annoyance for at times the ice would come up against the fuselage and the tidal water came on top of the ice.[5]

The men had cut holes in the ice that had frozen around the skis. Removing each undercarriage with the ski attached was difficult. Since a skin of ice would quickly form around the body of the plane, it had to be chipped off in successive stages as the plane was gradually levered up out of the water. However, they did succeed.

Once this had been accomplished, the black gang waited for the ice to become thick enough to support the use of a jack. Like their counterparts at Peechuk Point, they needed strong, stable ice. The mechanics were not idle during the wait, however, and continued to work on the engine. The propeller was removed from the engine, the engine dismantled, and all instruments disassembled. Working outside and with their bare hands, the group was exposed to increasingly colder temperatures and must have suffered intensely from the frigid Arctic air. The thinness of the ice made building any kind of fire too dangerous, and they could only thaw their freezing fingers by periodically burrowing their hands into the sleeves of their parkas. Not only were their hands frozen, but for the most part they stood in inches of icy water due to the action of the tide.[6] Cruickshank calculated the temperature with the wind chill at -43°C, as the one half-bottle of rum in his pocket had turned to slush. The air was metallic with the smell of cold and freezing water, and the sounds of hammering and clanging echoed across the inlet. They didn't discuss their discomforts. All the men knew and understood that time saved in the biting cold would get them back into the air much sooner and could mean the difference between life and death for the men they were seeking.

Inside the house at the Dominion Explorers' base, mechanics worked to remove any trace of damage from the action of the water. They baked the magnetos in the oven for two days and thoroughly inspected each and every piece of the Pratt and Whitney engine. The force of the plane going through the ice had bent the propeller, so Siers decided to shorten both propeller blades by four-and-a-half inches.[7] After this task, the propeller needed to be balanced. Shortened propeller blades would have a definite impact on the performance of 'SQ, but with Cruickshank's experience, he felt that he could handle the plane.[8]

While the engine was being repaired, the ice finally became firm enough to begin working on the aircraft. This would involve a tremendous amount of ingenuity. The tail of the plane was jacked up and placed on a fuel drum. Then the men took a three-by-six-inch piece of timber and placed it across the front of the undercarriage fittings of 'SQ. Once this was done they placed the jack (the only one they had) under the centre of the timber and raised the plane. Fuel drums were placed under the wings of the aircraft for support. Now the plane was exposed so that the undercarriage could be attached.[9]

When the plane went through the ice, it sustained a rip in the side of the fuselage, and Cruickshank had to repair it before he could fly. He came up with an inventive plan for patching the tear in the freezing temperatures. During his time with the RCMP in the Yukon, Cruickshank had learned to heat rocks in a fire and then add them to a pot filled with water to boil and cook his food. He decided to use the same technique. After heating several rocks in a fire, he then placed them in a can close to the plane to heat the immediate area, without putting the plane in danger. Then he heated the glue in another can. While the glue warmed, Cruickshank stitched a washed flour sack to the side of the fuselage.[10] Once the glue had melted, he covered the patch with the sticky matter and with bare fingers worked the "dope" into the stitches and onto the patch. This proved to be most successful, and the patch cured, tightening the fabric to the fuselage of the plane.[11] There was still work to be done on 'SQ before it could be air tested, but Siers was pleased with the ground testing of the engine and remained confident that Cruickshank would be able to fly the plane out.

———

Meanwhile, confidence was certainly lacking at Peechuck Point. The men were barely hanging on, and their raw nerves were revealed in a most acute state. Charlie and Jimmie had not returned and the men ate the last of the dog food and made a pot of "hot chocolate" using a single teaspoon of cocoa to a kettle of water. Pearce commented that one of the men was in bad shape with numbness in his arm and finger and a twitchy eye. The colonel was certain that strain was at the root of the problem and he ordered "strong emergency dope" to be dispensed.[12] At 5:30 p.m. the colonel and Pearce crawled into bed. During the night, they lay in wakeful turmoil. Every hour or so the colonel got up to check on the patient.

> November 1, 1929
> Richard Pearce's Diary, Peechuck Point
>
> It is 6:00 am and all is well. Charlie just barged in, left us a package of tobacco and told us he had brought fresh fish, flour and more sugar. He has gone off to bed but has left some flour. We asked him about the trip across the straits and he and Jack said they would feed us up and push off tomorrow. Our pipes came out and up went a smoke barrage. This is the first tobacco we have had for several days. Last night was tough. The herrings did not go very well. Alice is making tea and has mixed some flour for bannocks. We haven't tasted flour for a long time. The bannock was good, although seal oil was used for grease. Charlie decided not to go to bed and came back to our igloo to tell us that the Eskimos at Dease Point heard an aeroplane but could not see it. We figured that must have been the day before yesterday, but are not sure.

Feasting began and anticipation ran high. Charlie told the group that he passed a very big polar bear during his return to

Peechuck Point. Polar bears are one of the greatest dangers to Arctic travellers since they are not choosy about food. Being the top predator on the ice, whatever they find they will eat, including humans. This would be another concern as they began their crossing, but the excitement remained. Charlie finally determined that the ice was strong enough and promised they would start for the Hudson's Bay Post at Cambridge Bay the next day. It seemed to be a lucky omen.

"Brodie" Boadway shared the information that it would also have been his wedding day, so after the feast the men toasted him with coffee before climbing onto their sleeping ledge. Despite trying to get a good night's rest in preparation for the next day's journey, few slept at all. Thankfully, the patient was feeling better and he would be able to make the trip.

Everything seemed to be falling into place.

SEVEN

Arrival at Cambridge Bay

October 30, 1929
Andy's Diary, Burnside River

*Dud weather, no flying today. Ice gave way under starboard
wing of SQ. Had to make rafts of barrels and block her up
again. Stripped down part of [the] engine and worked on
mags [magnetos] etc.*

At Burnside River work continued on 'SQ. Once the skis were
attached, the aircraft was hauled manually over to more stable shore
ice. A large tarpaulin was thrown over the plane's nose as a makeshift
hanger, and, since the ice had now become thick and stable, a stove
made from a small gas barrel was placed underneath it to heat the

area where the mechanics worked. The job of assembling the engine, instruments, and propeller were next. The generator was ruined and the instruments were not functioning after their immersion in the water, but the assembly went on despite this. Cruickshank proposed to fly without instruments — no compass, turn and bank gage, pressure gauges, speedometer (needed for correct takeoff speed), nor temperature gauge. He would fly on one magneto, since the second had been destroyed during its icy immersion.

The Fokker Super Universal had two magnetos, and the pilot always made sure both were functional prior to takeoff. One was essential and the second was for backup. If one magneto quit, the second would keep the engine running. An "engine out" was something no pilot wanted to experience, since his airplane would become a glider. Cruickshank would be flying without the reassurance of a second magneto.

While 'SQ was being repaired, Spence and crew in 'CZ continued to fly searches during the later days of October, but upon landing at the Burnside base on the 31st his undercarriage collapsed. The ordinary bolts, which had been used to attach the undercarriage and skis to the Fairchild 'CZ at Baker Lake, had sheared off during what was a particularly rough landing. Luckily, Siers applied his ingenuity and resourcefulness once again to come up with a creative fix.

The men at Burnside lifted Spence's plane and placed the wings on fuel drums. Then, using a Pratt and Whitney crowfoot cylinder nut wrench, the mechanics began to work. The wrench was cut into a perfect length, filed to the correct diameter, and driven into the struts where the bolt had broken. This new "bolt" was then riveted over with a piece of sheet metal.

The plane, once repaired, was being overhauled for another search, but while that was being done, a deafening crash echoed through the air. 'CZ dropped heavily onto the ice once more as the second bolt added at Baker Lake broke. The black gang performed the same repair to the undercarriage and after both bolts had been replaced the plane had no further trouble.[1]

Courtesy of Western Canada Aviation Museum.

Bill Spence examines the collapsed undercarriage of 'CZ, its cantilever support coming dangerously close to touching the ice, risking damage to the wing.

With all the work that was going on, Cruickshank commented, dryly, that planes flying in the Arctic should carry toboggans to assist in hauling tools and equipment around camp. His November 3–4, 1929, diary entry, written at Burnside River, recorded that: "'SO, 'CZ and 'SL made flights, 4 hrs 35 min, and filled in country between Ellis [Ellice] River and Coast. [The following day] three planes searched towards Coronation then southwest along Burnside River. Have flown 5,000 miles west of Pelly by search planes to date."

Clouds blocked the searchers from flying over the Cambridge Bay area and to the north coast of the Kent Peninsula. Instead, they flew in the direction that the weather permitted and scoured the area around Burnside Valley, then southward to the Back River. Although they were doing all that they could, Blanchet wrote in his log that he found the situation discouraging and his hopes for success were ebbing.[2] Throughout the weeks of the search, the rescuers had experienced the vagaries of the Arctic climate. Nature's hostility had been shown in full force, yet these tireless men were committed to do a job and made no complaints. Soon, however, the choice to continue the search would be out of their hands.

Whether they succeeded or failed, the men and their planes would need to fly back to Winnipeg before the worst of winter set in. Dwindling fuel supplies and daylight were also issues. Since the rescue operation had begun, each day had become shorter by seven minutes, so that the searchers and the Domex men had lost almost five hours of daylight since September 27. The sun rose at 9:30 a.m. only to set again before 4:00 p.m. The daylight they had was taking on the quality of milky-blue dusk, with the sky barely distinguishable from the earth. With the monochromatic landscape and the men being immobilized by clouds and continuously confronted with bone-chilling cold, it's easy to imagine how they could readily fall into frustration and despair. Yet they did not. Soon the Arctic darkness would take hold, and the sun would only be a soft pink glow to the south. As the daylight hours declined, so too did their options. The lengthening shadows of night only seemed to emphasize the loneliness of this barren place and the seeming futility of their mission.

———

On November 2, 1929, the Domex men and their Inuit guides began the crossing of the ice towards Cambridge Bay. In 1909, Robert Edwin Peary, the first European to reach the North Pole, described ice travel in this area. "Beyond the glacial fringe is the indescribable surface ... of the tidal crack, that zone of unceasing conflict between the heavy floating ice and the stationary glacial fringe ... Here the ice is smashed into fragments of all sizes and piled up into great pressure ridges parallel with the shore."[3] There is little to suggest that conditions had changed in the intervening years. The currents deep within the Arctic Ocean caused the newly frozen ice surface to vibrate and reopen. The surface was pitted and unstable, but with a sense of resolve the men began their long awaited journey, with the Inuit leading the way.

November 2, 1929
Pearce's Diary, Peechuck Point

What a tough day! We spent hour after hour trying
to pick a course through a large ice floe, wandering
this way and that to find the best going. Sleds were
tugged and pushed over ice hummocks that we
initially thought were impossible to cross. More
than once we tumbled into holes between ice cakes.
It was all nerve-wracking and tiring … Narrow
leads of unsafe ice had to be crossed, but before we
ventured on them the Eskimos tested them with
spears. Alice, the wife of the Eskimo with whom
the Colonel, Baker and I were traveling, took her
boy of three after he had been tossed from the sled
several times, stripped him naked and tied him
on her back under her clothing. This did not stop
her from continuing a man's share of the work of
urging the dogs and helping tug the sleds over the
most difficult spots … Once while crossing weak
ice, apparently frozen only the night before, she
broke through to her knees. Instead of trying to
scramble out — which would probably have meant
that she would sink deeper — she lay flat until one
of the Eskimos rescued her … Alice changed into
dry clothing out in the open without any apparent
great discomfort, although the temperature was
well below zero. At 4 p.m. we struck thin ice. The
Eskimos could find no way to cross it. It was then
a matter of parking for the night on an ice floe,
hoping that in the morning the going would be
safe. Some of the party feared that the strong wind
then blowing would carry the floe down the straits
and perhaps break it up.

Despite opposition, the Inuit sensibly called a halt to the trek. Thousands of years in the North had taught them the wisdom of survival even when it meant delays. Shelter was a priority. Igloos needed to be built to protect the group from the biting wind. During construction, Pearce's frozen moccasins slipped and he crashed into the side of an igloo, causing it to collapse. The normally patient Inuits' tempers were also starting to fray. New blocks needed to be cut and it wasn't long before the weary group was settled down for a very nerve-racking night on the ice floe.

The powerful movement of the Arctic Ocean current, called the Beaufort Gyre, was at work beneath the little camp. Below the shivering men, the ice also shivered. Moving ice is dangerous ice, and, with nothing under them but frigid water up to thousands of feet deep, should a lead (crack) in the ice pack reopen without warning, everything would be swallowed into the black depths below. This was not the only way they could die on the ice. The active current working under them could carry the group on their small chunk of ice further away from Cambridge Bay. Ice floes have been known to travel up to twelve miles per night. Not only would they lose what progress they had achieved, but also their chances of staying alive since their food rations were so limited. These terrors were not far from their minds.

The dogs were another concern. These animals had worked as hard, if not harder, than the men and they needed attention. Driving dogs requires a fine balance and it is not for amateurs. The Eskimo dog has been bred by the Inuit to go for long periods of time without food, but the harder the dogs are pushed, the greater the risk of burnout. This made it essential to keep the dogs motivated, not only through encouragement, but also thorough scrupulous attention and care. Paws had to be checked throughout the day for any snow buildup or cuts from shards of sharp ice. As the Polar explorer Tom Avery wrote, the willingness of these animals to continue running through such a desperate environment may just put a human's suffering and discomfort into perspective.[4] After all, the dogs slept outdoors.

Courtesy of Daryl Goodwin.

Bright-eyed and ready to go, the huskies wait for direction.

All through that night the ice cracked and groaned with its piercing, almost haunting sounds of agony. The men were agitated and restless. Despite exhaustion, sleep did not come easily. All were aware that death is a natural companion in the North, yet none dared mention the very real possibility that a lead would take the little group whole into the jaws of the Arctic Ocean abyss. No matter how well prepared they were or how carefully they planned, nature had the ultimate control.

———

In the fading light at Burnside River, the rescue team was facing critical decisions. With limited fuel remaining, the search could only continue with dog teams led by members of Dominion Explorers from the Burnside base, while the pilots and their crews would head back to Winnipeg. To end like this was devastating. Throughout the search the pilots and their engineers had remained optimistic. Through wind, ice, and snow they had battled over rugged terrain, waited out storms, made repairs to their aircraft, all the while searching the Barren Lands and along the Arctic coastline for thousands of miles. Yet now it was to end, but not because of weather or lack of optimism. It was a business decision.

Cruickshank decided that they would fly one more search on November 5, weather permitting, and then begin the flights back home as instructed by Brintnell. This was a difficult pill for the men to swallow. They had been risking their lives over the past several weeks to save those of MacAlpine and his men, but Western Canada Airways was getting impatient, and they wanted their planes back on normal routes. The company had been losing revenue with their fleet of aircraft engaged in the search. The harshness of the situation was apparent. Physically the men were able to endure, at least for a little longer, but they had no choice but to listen to the manager of WCA. Ironically, they were being torn out of the North for the same kind of financial reason that had propelled the Dominion Explorers into the Barren Lands so late in the season.

The sky on November 4 was black and unreadable. There was heaviness among the men as they sat down for dinner, possibly for the last time before they would pack up to head back Outside. The gloomy weather was mirrored in the men's grim expressions. There were no card games to lighten the spirits. Instead they focused on their last search, which would be towards the Coppermine River, one of the destinations planned on the Domex route.

———

Just one day earlier the Domex men and their Inuit companions had made themselves ready to attempt the crossing. They had not slept. With the security of stable land a distant memory, they had listened to the cacophony of hammering and scraping as the ice shuddered beneath them, propelled by shockwaves all night long.

November 3 was a frigid day, with a temperature measuring -33°C. After breakfast they loaded the sleds and harnessed the dogs. Their only concern was being able to cross the perilous ice as quickly as possible. Here patience would not be an asset.

As Peary said, "A man who should wait for the ice to be really safe would stand small chance of getting far in these latitudes. Traveling on the polar ice, one takes all kinds of chances. Often a man has the choice between the possibility of drowning by going on or starving to death by standing still."[5]

Sea ice, with its high salt content, is the most flexible of any type of ice. Fresh water, when frozen, sets like glass, but a thin layer of frozen seawater has a rubbery consistency and flexes under any type of weight, be it a plane, human, sled, or dog. On this undulating surface they were off and running, and within minutes the air pierced their lungs as they gasped for oxygen. Breath curdled heavily on the fur of their parkas, and soon there was an inch of frost covering their clothing. Sweat-soaked garments became an icy armour, but nonetheless they ran. Conditions were deplorable, their vision suffering, and yet they ran and ran in a vast, icy cloud, making their way around ice hummocks. All while the ice was moving under their feet.

Polar explorers have written of the strange optical illusion that occurs at the frozen ends of the earth. The whiteout is a phenomenon that even at mid-day may prevent a man from seeing dangers right at his feet.[6] In total whiteness depth perception is lost. Conditions like this made the crossing shockingly unreal; the horizon disappeared and the men lost all orientation. They continued the race of their lives, with an icy blast gnawing at them and a desperate determination to survive.

They suffered intensely. The jagged ice upset the sleds time and again and the dreaded ice hummocks forced them well off course. Collapsing fragile ice caused them to stumble and fall, and arms and legs felt like they were being torn loose from their joints. Violent trembling from sheer exhaustion seemed to beat the life back in them, or perhaps they were pushed by the necessity to get out of the wind and fine snow that continually bit at them. The two groups lost sight of each other and the first team disappeared into the white nothingness. Waiting for the second to catch up was not an option. Each footstep was one closer to Cambridge, or so they hoped, but each one more painful than the last. They continued placing one foot in front of the other thousands upon thousands of times. Mind and spirit dissolved and they ran on pure adrenaline. Their only awareness was of sound — panting dogs, groaning ice, crunching footsteps, and their ragged, rasping breath.

With the exception of the exhausted colonel, who rode on one of the sleds for part of the way, the group raced across the wavering ice that was pitted with porous, green slushy spots. Pearce wrote that his second wind passed without recognition and he was on his fifth by mile two. Toes, faces, and fingers were frozen. Surface water worked its way into their footwear, and socks were soon frozen to their moccasins. The twelve miles stretched into thirty as they worked their way around the floe ice, but they dared not stop.

The last thirty-mile dash over barely frozen sea ice from Dease Point to Cambridge Bay was successful — the moment the men had longed for! Hope had turned into realization. The first Domex team arrived ice-shelled and sweat-soaked alongside the *Baymaud*, the ship that Roald Amundsen had used for his Arctic exploration in 1918. Pearce was in this group and his anxiety about being taken in because he smelled of seal oil was dispelled. The residents at Cambridge were the first English-speaking Europeans they had seen in fifty-six days, and these hospitable and kind people gave no indications that the smell of seal oil was anything but normal. Emotions ran high — a

Provincial Archives of Manitoba, Canadian Air Lines Collection #2130.

A weary and motley Dominion Explorer expedition arrives at the Baymaud.

mingling of exhaustion, elation, relief, and gratitude. A combination of reuniting with those who had been aware of the lost party and the world-wide attention the search and rescue had received humbled the men. All of a sudden they were thrown into the spotlight of fame and glory, all of which was unnerving. Along with joy were doubts and fears — the second team had not yet arrived at Cambridge Bay.

It was a worrying next few hours as the group waited for the second set of travellers. In their physically exhausted state, the new arrivals were almost sick with apprehension. Some wanted to leave the sanctuary of the settlement and go out and search for them, but the unstable ice conditions rendered this impossible. Darkness, both physical and emotional, began to grip the small community. The first team feared the worst, thinking their colleagues had been swallowed into the abyss — how could they have become separated and left them out there?

Finally, three hours later, the anxiously awaited second team pulled alongside the *Baymaud* and was greeted with joy, solicitude, and hot food, in that order.[7] The inhabitants of Cambridge Bay were only too happy to accommodate the weary group. The Hudson's Bay men, RCMP members, and Canalaska[8] trading staff, began serving up potatoes, jam, marmalade, bread, cake, and cheese. Euphoria permeated the air at Cambridge Bay as all indulged in the much-deserved celebrating.

For the first time in almost two months, the Domex men slept on beds with clean sheets and blankets. Each household community welcomed two or three men. Don Goodwin and Tommy Thompson stayed at the Hudson's Bay house with Mr. and Mrs. George Clark; Alex Milne, E.A. Boadway, and Stan McMillan were with Corporal Frank Belcher and Constable Robert Milne of the RCMP; and Colonel MacAlpine, Major Baker, and Richard Pearce were on the *Baymaud*, attended to by Ian McKinnon and Mat Shand. The Inuit were swiftly building igloos this night, no doubt delighted to be on stable land. Food was served continuously, to the great relief of both the Domex men and the Inuit and their exhausted and very hungry dog teams. Inside or out, everyone slept like the dead.

Fittingly, MacAlpine and Pearce stayed aboard the schooner. The Hudson's Bay Company had purchased the *Baymaud* three years earlier and she had sailed from Vancouver to Cambridge Bay in June 1926 and had remained there — frozen in the ice. The *Baymaud* had been used variously as a machine shop, storage facility, and wireless station from 1926–27. During that time she transmitted weather reports, the first sent by radio from Canada's Arctic coast. But, unfortunately, in 1929, the wireless had not been in operation for over two years. Now MacAlpine and Pearce were finding refuge on this very same ship.

The colonel wrote messages for Pearce to type on the *Baymaud*'s typewriter to be sent to family, Western Canada Airways, and the Dominion Explorers' headquarters. Every time Pearce's frostbitten fingers struck the keys pain shot through him, but he persisted with the task, knowing that the information would be of great relief to family and friends.

November 3, 1929
Pearce's Diary, Cambridge Bay

After midnight came the first real bed since August 25th, with something soft underneath the body and a covering of dry, clean blankets. Just before going to bed, the Colonel, Bob and I cleaned up three tins of tomatoes. Mat Shand, in charge of the Baymaud, told us that all the Colonel had eaten for supper was six eggs, a liberal helping of bacon, bread and other things, and three-quarters of a raisin pie. His second meal at the Hudson [sic] Bay house later in the evening was equally modest… half-way through the night, Baker and I awoke, had another meal, and to help pass the time, this diary was resumed. Then I climbed into Bob's bunk and we ate a pound of chocolates between us.

Courtesy of Western Canada Aviation Museum.

Standing on the ice alongside the Baymaud *in Cambridge Bay, with the Domex men eagerly await pickup. This was a long-anticipated day!*

The messages were given to Ian McKinnon, the Hudson's Bay Company's clerk aboard the *Baymaud*. He immediately set up his small amateur radio using the high masts of the schooner as aerial hook-up to send the great news of the safe arrival of the MacAlpine group to the Outside. He was unable to make contact with Winnipeg, Toronto, or family members. Fortunately, the faint message he kept trying to send was picked up by Ross Smythe, a McGill University student and the wireless operator living aboard the Hudson's Bay Company's SS *Fort James* at Gjoa Haven on King Wiliam Island, about 315 miles away. Smythe then sent the messages to the Outside.

On November 4, an anxiously awaiting country heard, "MacAlpine and party found. All well. Located Cambridge Bay."[9] A nation rejoiced.

The Northern Miner's front-page edition printed the news on November 7, 1929. The story captured the highlights of the extraordinary adventure and told of the harsh conditions, including bone-chilling gales, meagre food supplies, struggles against physical weakness, and loss of weight. And yet the Dominion Explorers had made their way to safety, high above the Arctic Circle with a very happy outcome. The story also praised the search and rescue pilots for their determination during the search and praised them for the advancement they have made in opening the North. The story claimed that the men had shown the Arctic could be conquered!

The news now had to reach the searchers at Burnside River before they began the flight south from the Arctic. The SS *Fort James* had a large radio set, and Smythe became the messenger sending word to anxious families, Dominion Explorers company officials, the media, and the Hudson's Bay Company Hood Trading Post at Bathurst Inlet.

Once the Hood Trading Post picked up the message from Smythe, it was sent to Colonel James K. Cornwall, a field manager who had established the Dominion Explorers base at Burnside in 1928. When the good news reached Bathurst, Cornwall was at a camp about thirty miles south of Bathurst Inlet. The message was sent on to him and he immediately sent Kingmeak (an Inuit runner with him at the time) and his dog team to Burnside River to inform Cruickshank.[10] Kingmeak travelled the distance in ten hours, racing through the Arctic night to reach the Burnside base at 7:30 in the morning. He arrived just as the planes were being warmed up for their last search flight.[11] Kingmeak shouted above the engine roar "They fine 'em! They fine 'em!"[12] He passed a piece of paper to one of the waiting searchers. It read, "Schooner Fort James at the Magnetic Pole reports message from the *Baymaud* at Cambridge Bay on November third that the lost party had arrived there on this date from Dease Point."[13] The searchers Cruickshank and his men were elated.

The economically driven decisions to return the planes from the Arctic would, instead, become a humanitarian flight, bringing the lost men back to civilization. Brintnell would get his planes back and the rescuers would succeed in their quest. The rescue pilots changed their flight plan to head to Cambridge Bay via the Hood Trading Post to pick up the Dominion Explorers and begin their evacuation from the Barrens. From there it would be a four-day trip back to Winnipeg.

But the force of nature that, according to *The Northern Miner* had been "conquered," had other plans for the intruders of its territory.

| EIGHT |

Evacuation Planning

November 5, 1929
Andy Cruickshank's Diary, Burnside River, Arctic Circle

At 7:30, a native arrived just as machines were ready to leave. Bringing news that the lost party were at Cambridge Bay. Machines immediately left for Cambridge Bay.

'SL, 'SO, and 'CZ, all of which had been fuelled and warmed up for the search towards the Coppermine, taxied out on the ice, and took off for Hood Trading Post. The post was north of Burnside River and offered a location that would give the planes a head start to Cambridge Bay the following morning. Getting away as soon as the sun rose in the Arctic sky was important, since the pilots, crew, and weary travellers would need a quick turnaround from Cambridge Bay to head southward before darkness. Since there was a wireless at the HBC Hood Post, the searchers could be in communication with Mat Shand aboard the *Baymaud* at Cambridge Bay and get accurate and updated weather forecasts.

The three planes landed at the trading post, and each aircraft waddled over the rolling snow contours. The sound of the motors broke through the stillness, humming where the surface was smooth, and growling where extra power was required to climb a drift. Once the planes came to a stop and the engines had been shut down the men were welcomed into the post for the evening.

It was only once there that Spence, Hollick-Kenyon, Brown, and their crews heard about the media reports that had captivated both national and international attention for the past months. Reports were in all the major newspapers and been broadcast over radio stations for weeks, and now congratulations were pouring in from all over North America. The news, however, did not travel in a straight line, nor very quickly. These messages were going via the *Fort James* at Gjoa Haven, then phoned in to Cambridge Bay, and forwarded to the Hood Trading Post. Optimism had remained high that the Domex men would be found alive, but divine intervention was also welcome — even churches as far away as Salt Lake City were broadcasting prayers for the safety of the "brave Arctic fliers."[1] When word finally reached Outside, relief on both sides of the 49th parallel was palpable. It was at the Hudson Bay's post that the searchers heard of the Great Stock Market Crash, which had occurred on October 29, 1929, less than a week before.

Energized by skyrocketing stock prices of the early fall of 1929, the Domex prospectors had left to scour the Arctic for minerals, which would in time possibly become mines. In their absence, the country and the rest of the industrial world economy had begun a collapse on a scale never before seen. MacAlpine's Dominion Explorers stock had tumbled from its $14.67 share price to a mere 50 cents since Colonel MacAlpine's disappearance. Despite this drastic plunge, on the whole, Canada's economy would in fact be somewhat cushioned from the disasters that befell other countries because of the insightful vision of the founders of Domex. Dominion Explorers' Falconbridge and Eldorado Silver were two mining developments, whose success during the Depression would help support Canada's economic stability through that dark period.

The newcomers to Hood Post were stunned by the events that had been unfolding during the last few days. They couldn't help but wonder what the future held for a bush pilot. However, daily "news" often lost its significance during time spent in the Barrens. In this harsh landscape a person's relationship with nature is far more intimate than news of events, however cataclysmic, in distant Outside cities. Living by the rhythms of the land required their attention to the present moment rather than being distracted by news that was out of date by the time it reached them. The men turned their concentration once more to the job at hand, then rested up for the flight out to Cambridge Bay scheduled for daybreak.

Cruickshank, although remaining at Burnside to complete the repairs on 'SQ, had organized the airlift out of Cambridge Bay. He arranged for the Domex men to be divided between the bases at Bathurst and Burnside River until plans had been finalized for the trip Outside. The plan would prevent overcrowding at both locations and give the Dominion Explorers more spacious accommodations and much-needed extra food.

Since responsibility for both the safety of the aircraft and the route out rested on Cruickshank, he began his thoughtful evacuation planning. He was reluctant to head south via Hudson Bay due to its shroud of fog banks that could rest on the waters for days on end. He preferred to go out through Fort Reliance and Cranberry Portage, even though this route would take the airmen and their passengers over the open waters of Great Slave Lake, a concern since the planes were ski-equipped. But this route would also take the pilots further away from Baker Lake, where Vance and

Blasdale were awaiting parts for the damaged 'RK. He mulled this over while continuing to assist with the engine assembly of 'SQ.

———

At Cambridge Bay, waiting for evacuation plans to unfold, the Domex men could finally assess their health situation. They were frostbitten and malnourished. During their weeks of limited food intake and caloric shortfall, their bodies had begun to digest themselves, drawing on precious fat reserves in an attempt to stay alive, which, in turn, reduced their tolerance to the cold. That, compounded with extreme physical activity and dehydration, resulted in a susceptibility to poor circulation. Also, since the body's natural tendency is to pull blood from the extremities towards the heart and lungs, supplying them with critical nutrients, if permanently constricted, the cells in these blood vessels could burst and form small clots.

All the men suffered from frostbite to some degree, but it became apparent that Don Goodwin was in serious condition. Both feet were frozen, one worse than the other. There was the very real possibility that he might lose it. During the last night on the ice, Goodwin had not mentioned his footgear was soaked through. He had continued to run with the rest of the group, without referring to the condition of his feet when they settled on the ice floe. This lack of comment may have been a result of severe frostbite. Once frostbite has penetrated to the third layer of the skin, feeling is lost in that area. There have been reports that an area "bitten" hard feels wooden. Pearce, however, once he saw Goodwin's white-purple foot, recalled the anguished look on Goodwin's face as they made their final thirty-mile dash, and noted in his diary that he had wished that Goodwin had made mention of his discomfort. It was urgent that Goodwin be seen by a doctor.

The other members of the team had frostbitten fingertips and noses, and the average weight of the men was 110 pounds, down from 150 pounds. Colonel MacAlpine had lost seventy pounds.[2]

Scurvy was another problem. Their teeth were loose and in desperate shape with fillings falling out due to the diet they had been forced to eat for the past two months. With attentive care and good food the men began to regain their strength, although their stomachs reacted violently to the food they were now eating. This back to normal diet was supplemented by vast quantities of Scotch. In two days the eight men helped to consume Cambridge Bay's year's supply of alcohol.

Most of the members of the team relaxed while they waited for an airlift out. The Inuit women washed and scrubbed the men's clothing and hung them to dry in the various houses at Cambridge Bay. Major Baker even managed to have a bath, the first one in two months.

The colonel continued to keep Pearce busy writing and sending messages to the Outside. He sent a wire to the Dominion Explorers headquarters in Toronto:

> All personnel both planes safe STOP Please rush advice all concerned STOP Subsequent to leaving Lake Pelly a chapter of unlucky incidents including snow storm and no safe landing forced us far north of our course and landing at first opportunity unanimous decision account gas supply was to hit for Arctic coast STOP We landed at Eskimo Tent in vicinity Dease Point and again on account unfortunate incident combined gas supply insufficient for one plane to reach trading post STOP All other plans to reach post proved futile on account open seas STOP There was no alternative but to wait until we could reach Cambridge Bay over ice on the sea STOP With bitter disappointment but with resignation to the inevitable we began the fight for food and preparations against the climate and have just reached Cambridge Bay over the ice STOP Overshadowing our own troubles was the

worry of those at home and hazards of those who
might blindly search for us STOP Official report
of details will follow…. MacALPINE

In his communications role, Pearce had heard about the
various searches that would be implemented once the air search
had been called off and the search planes headed south. An Inuit
communication line had been set up by Colonel Cornwall,
manager at the Hood Trading Post at Bathurst Inlet. He had
promised a hefty reward to the Inuit who was able to provide news
of the lost Domex men. Cornwall had heard rumours from the
Inuit of planes heading over the Ellice River areas and wanted to
get information himself from the Inuit settlements. He also had
wired the RCMP at Cambridge Bay to send dog teams along the
Queen Maud Gulf (on the northern coast of Nunavut) as soon as
the ice was stable to investigate the possibility of the men being
stranded somewhere on the Gulf shores. Pearce later learned that
the crossing Dominion Explorers made on November 3 was one of
the earliest ever recorded since Europeans had arrived in the North.

While waiting for the rescue aircraft to arrive from Burnside,
Pearce had contacted his brother Norman, a co-owner and co-editor
at *The Northern Miner*. Richard wired the story of their dramatic
journey out to Norman for distribution to the media. Norman
sold the story for $10,000 to *The Star* in Toronto and Pearce had
the money divided among the Domex men, who were thrilled
with their share. Richard Pearce was also offered $5 per word
from, it seemed, almost every newspaper in the country.[3] With this
kind of encouragement, he continued with his correspondence
despite blood blisters on his fingertips. With the assistance of Ian
McKinnon, Pearce was doing his best to reply to the incoming
messages. The task seemed endless, but it was one he was skilled
at, unlike building sod houses. Pearce did, however, decide to take
some time away from the typewriter to view the spectacular show
of the northern lights from the deck of the *Baymaud*.

Others were watching this impressive display. From the ice at Burnside, Cruickshank gazed skyward at the aurora borealis. No matter how often he was treated to this incredible light display, he always stopped to appreciate it. As he watched, he thought of Esmé, as he knew she was just as awestruck as he when the brilliant lights began to dance. The silhouette of 'SQ against the light display was a stark contrast, and very modern, considering that aircraft had never been part of that world before. As he stood beside his plane and watched the lights sweeping the heavens, a sense of foreboding weighed heavily on his mind. The flights home, he feared, would be far from straightforward.

Weather was a constant question mark — fierce winds, fog banks, snow squalls, and extreme cold were ever-present threats. Fuel was nearly spent. Added to this was the burden of knowing that this was their last opportunity to see their mission through. Faced with these concerns and this undercurrent of dread, he knew how important meticulous planning was to their success. He knew what the Arctic demanded. A hurried dash south would not be in the best interest of the people whose safety was his responsibility.

His own plane alone was going to be a particular challenge for him to fly, but this he felt he could control. He would be flying without instruments, with a shortened propeller, and on one magneto. Siers, along with Cruickshank, had discussed the effects these emergency alterations to his plane would have on the safety, horsepower, and overall performance of the aircraft. They also discussed the weight capacity of the 'SQ. Siers doubted 'SQ could handle more than two passengers. This would present a difficulty in itself, getting all the passengers safely back to Winnipeg with four planes and one only able to fly with two passengers in as short a time as possible. From what Cruickshank had heard over the wireless, a total of twenty-two men needed flights back home as there were other passengers wanting a ride from the Bathurst Base.

He contemplated calling in any available planes for assistance, but decided to wait to discuss with MacAlpine.

Mists closed in on the morning of November 6. The rescue planes sat at Hood Post, waiting for a break in the weather. It was an agonizing wait. The moment the mist cleared, the air engineers readied the planes and they were off, heading immediately for Cambridge Bay. Minutes later, they left the brilliant sunshine and flew into a cloudbank resting at ground level and were forced to land.[4] Landing blind, pilots and passengers were thrown from one side of the aircraft to the other as the planes struggled for stability. They waited for the skies to clear with engines running, consuming precious fuel.

Suddenly, a wind blew in from the north and cleared the fog. They were off again. Circling over the Queen Maud Gulf, they were dismayed to see ice floes piled haphazardly in such confusion that the three planes had no clear area for landing. They continued flying and finally located a smooth strip of ice between one of the many islands and the shore. They landed right near dog-sled tracks, which they suspected must have been made by the Dominion Explorers three days before. They waited again — so close to their destination of Cambridge Bay but pinned to the earth by the Arctic's atmospheric moods.

Once the clouds dissipated for the third time, the area was bathed in sunlight. Tiny ice crystals picked up by the fresh wind twinkled like magical dust, showing a softer side of this harsh environment. Into this crystal sky flew Hollick-Kenyon and Brown. But in his haste to take off, Spence forgot to select his full fuel tank. The aircraft the bush pilots were flying were equipped with two fuel tanks, one in each wing. The typical procedure was to run one tank dry at high altitude, allowing a switch over to the other full tank to maximize the range. Take-off was usually done on the fuller tank. Fifty feet up, Spence's engine cut and he was heading straight for Cape Colbourn Cliff. He had no choice but to hold his course and glide, hoping for the best. A pilot has very few options over an aircraft with an engine out at fifty feet. Bill Spence and Guy Blanchet watched in horror as the snow-swept rocky cliff loomed in the cockpit window.

Unaware of their colleagues' harrowing situation, Hollick-Kenyon and Brown arrived at Cambridge Bay without mishap. When the red flags flapping above the *Baymaud* came into view, both pilots lined up a landing path and came to stop adjacent to the Hudson's Bay Post. Once the engines were throttled down, men from everywhere, it seemed, rushed onto the ice to greet the long-awaited rescue pilots, their voices echoing over the pitted surface of the ice. It was then that Hollick-Kenyon noticed that Spence in 'CZ was missing.

Finally Spence and Blanchet arrived. Spence, using his flying skills masterfully, had been able to land his plane just a few feet from the base of Colbourn Cliff. After taking some time to reassess his narrow escape from death and wait for the adrenaline to subside, Spence switched fuel tanks and took off again. He and Blanchet breathed a sigh of relief as Cambridge Bay came into

The rescue planes 'SO and 'SL pull along side the Baymaud ready to load the Domex men for their flight south. The Fokker Super Universal could carry six passengers and two crewmembers, along with gear.

view. This landing was much calmer. He taxied along the bumpy ice and cut his engine beside the *Baymaud*. Once out of the plane, Blanchet took control. He divided the eight Domex men into the waiting aircraft. Goodwin, whose feet were still too damaged to support him, was piggy-backed to the aircraft.

Before boarding, the men said their goodbyes to their Inuit friends with mixed feelings. One of them commented, "If we had been their own children, they could not have 'mothered' us with greater care. When luxuries such as tobacco, tea, and sugar ran low, they shared their last with us. When rations ran out in our igloo at Kent Peninsula, they shared their meagre store with us. Even our lack of suitable clothing, a cause of grave discomfort, they did their best to supply."[5] It was an emotional farewell, but the men were keen to start the flight back Outside to their loved ones and the lives they had left behind. Despite the rotten food, the primitive uncomfortable shelter, and the abuses of nature, it was a wrench to leave the Inuit behind. In all likelihood, the Domex men would never see their Inuit benefactors again.

Climbing aboard 'SO, 'SL, and 'CZ, they settled themselves and refocused on the next step in the journey. The pilots polished their skis and then taxied across the bumpy ice until they reached takeoff speed. Blanchet wrote in his log that he noticed the unmistakable signs of strain and privation on the faces of the men and that they were all suffering from a nervous reaction to their ordeal.[6]

On the flight to Bathurst Inlet, Pearce wrote about the relief that was felt as the men took to the sky. Passing back over their route from Kent Peninsula, to Peechuck Point, to Dease Point in the distance, he couldn't help but be awestruck at the distance travelled over such difficult and harsh terrain.

Hollick-Kenyon with MacMillan, Boadway, and Milne arrived at Burnside River around 4:30 p.m. Brown and Spence, carrying MacAlpine, Pearce, Baker, Goodwin, and Thompson, stayed at Hood Trading Post for the night. The space was tight, yet once again food and genuine hospitality were expansive. Brown and his passengers had planned to head to Burnside but poor weather changed his mind, and he turned his plane around and joined the others at Hood Post. Banter took hold at the very small post, and the men wrote a poem to commemorate the events of the past few months.

"To the Flying Sourdoughs"

Oh, we came up from Winnipeg
Where the old Red River flows
We all came up to Bathurst
Because we love you so.
So if you're still at Cambridge
Just write and let us know
And we'll come up and get you
Because we love you so.

The stanzas continued in rhyme, giving the routes taken by the rescue team. The area searched was astounding: Dubawnt River, Baker Lake, Pelly, Bathurst, Ellice River, and, according to the poets, "from the north plum to the south." Expounding on the harsh winter conditions, they suggested, none to kindly, a place where the Arctic Circle could go. They ended their poetic song with:

For we could not spot an igloo
From a good three thousand feet
It doesn't look like Portage Ave.
Or Winnipeg's main street.
Oh, eight men in a sod hut
Is not such easy meat
To attract a plane's attention
Get off your blasted seat.

According to the January 23, 1930, edition of *The Northern Miner*, very few verses could be printed without setting the presses on fire! The night continued with further poetic banter:

Far, far from Burnside I long to be
Where the northwester can't get at me:
Cold is my eiderdown, cold are my feet
Ten howling huskies to wail me to sleep.
The north wind's still blowing,
Our engines are cold:
All skis are frozen,
And we're getting old.
Small are my mukluks,
Swollen my feet;
Doc thinks it's scurvy.
And feeds us raw meat.

The second poem describes their ordeal in comic form once again. By the content, one might think that alcohol had taken effect. The "poets" expounded on the antics of the dog teams, the frozen components of the aircraft, and the wind — oh the wind! They carry on describing the physical affects and what "Doc" recommends. One can only hope that after their descriptive verse sung to an old-time melody, "Sing me to Sleep," they fell into a deep slumber.

With space so crowded, there were two settings for meals, and to accommodate the sleepers on the floor, chairs and gear were piled on top of the stove and table. The following morning Roy Brown took off for Burnside River with Major Thompson, Major Baker, and Don Goodwin. Once the latter arrived his feet would be examined by Dr. Bruce. Goodwin's frostbitten feet were recovering, yet an amputation and the attendant risks of infection and gangrene were very real fears. It was imperative to get him back to Winnipeg as quickly as possible.

MacAlpine was making arrangements for the Hudson's Bay manager at the Bathurst Post to take care of their Inuit rescuers. He arranged for clothing, rifles, ammunition, tobacco, cigarettes, cigarette papers, and hand-sewing machines to be given to the group, and left several hundred dollars at the post for anything the Inuit might need at a later date. It was impossible to repay them, the colonel felt. A life cannot be measured in cash or in items from a trading post, but he wanted to make sure that these very special people would have everything they needed, but, reflecting the stereotypical thinking of the era, without "spoiling them, [or] keeping them from working for a few years, which would be the unkindest thing we could do."[7] These people were their lifelines, and the Domex men could not do enough for them in appreciation for their having kept them alive.

Indeed, as Tommy Thompson said, "No account of our stay at Dease Point could be complete without an eulogy on the Eskimo. He is probably considered a heathen by the churches but personally I have never met truer Christians nor more truthful, honest, generous people."[8] Thompson's appreciation of Inuit generosity was not reflected in his own behavior, however.

November 7, 1929
Andy Cruickshank's Diary, Burnside River

Spence and Brown returned this A.M. [They] had stayed over night at H.B. Post. Brought Thompson, Goodwin [and] Baker. Goodwin suffering from frozen feet. All others have a slight touch of scurvy. SQ engine almost finished. Siers and crew working from daylight till 9 P.M. Asked Thompson to let us take his elevators and rudder [from the SK at Dease Point] to Vance but he won't hear of it. [There have been] big arguments about route out. I am in favor of Reliance if we cannot take Vance any spares.

Cruickshank was not happy with the response from Thompson. The flight from Burnside River to Dease Point was within easy distance and parts from the stranded Fokker 'SK at Dease Point could repair the damaged Fokker 'RK at Baker Lake and allow Vance and Blasdale to return with the rescue planes. With Thompson's refusal, Vance and Blasdale would have to remain at Baker Lake for the winter until replacement parts could be sent from Winnipeg, and with the onset of winter this would not happen until breakup in the late spring. Cruickshank repeatedly tried to convince Thompson but failed. Even though Cruickshank had been given responsibility of the air search, he had to accept Thompson's refusal, as Thompson held a more senior position with Western Canada Airways. With nothing more to be accomplished on this topic, attention then turned to the flight out using the four remaining planes.

One route discussed was to cross the Barrens, continuing to Baker Lake, then on to Churchill, where the Domex men would board the train to Winnipeg. Weather was a definite concern with this route, although it would mean that Vance and Blasdale could be picked up, rather than being left for the winter. The second, and the shorter route, was to Fort Reliance, a Domex base at the east end of Great Slave Lake. From there they would fly on towards Stony Rapids, Cranberry Portage, and finally to Winnipeg.[9]

Eventually, Cruickshank decided to take the shorter route, avoiding the Barrens and the challenging weather patterns over Hudson Bay. Jim Vance and B.C. Blasdale would have to mush out using a dog team and sled, which would take them months, or else wait until parts and tools could be sent in the spring. Wireless messages were sent to Winnipeg and Toronto notifying headquarters of their plans.

The estimated time of travel was four days. However, Cruickshank's premonition was correct, and the journey would be far longer.

| NINE |

Airborne to Fort Reliance

"Any news of the Fliers?" The anxious query has echoed and re-echoed in Canadian homes ever since the MacAlpine party was first reported missing. Their enterprise had caught and uplifted the national imagination, and as day followed day without any news of them, hope deferred cast its pall of gloom over the entire Dominion. Then came the wonderful news: "Fliers safe at Cambridge Bay!" It was a glorious climax to a great adventure — and now Canada testifies how keen was her anxiety in a spontaneous expression of relief and gratitude for their rescue. As she gives thanks for many material blessings, Canada adds with fervent voice: "Thank God the fliers are safe!"

The Manitoba Free Press, *November 11, 1929*

An invisible bond between Canadians and their dauntless aviation heroes and adventurous explorers was strengthened even more. The spirit of resourcefulness, integrity, compassion for others, and resilience was the foundation of Canadian character, one that would be admired and respected and repeated through future generations. The rescue had all the hallmarks of this quality. Emotions ran high as people prepared to welcome their champions home.

Unaware of their status, the "champions" had completed repairs on 'SQ and flights home could begin. Siers and the black gang's work had been remarkably successful, and the test flight Cruickshank took left him feeling confident he could fly safely back to Winnipeg. Despite a nagging feeling in the pit of his stomach about the return, he looked forward to the flight home. What this feeling did, however, was to make him more cautious with each decision. His RCMP training had ingrained in his character a thoroughness and discipline that would serve them well.

On November 11, all members of the Domex group and the additional passengers assembled at Burnside River, with the departure date set for the 12th. Within hours they would be embarking on a 2,000-mile flight in three "hops" to Winnipeg. On November 12, 1929, *The Manitoba Free Press* reported the following: "[On] Andy Cruickshank rests the responsibility of the decision when engine fitness and weather conditions favor the resumption of the journey home. Cruickshank has charge of the flights."

It was with great relief that the pilots, engineers, and passengers welcomed November 12. The day dawned with clear skies and a good wind for takeoff. Conditions could not be more favourable for Arctic flying. Cruickshank had discussed the flight path with the other pilots and suggested flying in formation. This would enable all the pilots and passengers to be on the lookout for potential hazards, such as incoming bad weather or open waterways.

Fort Reliance would be the first stop, and they would need to find a suitable place to land the four planes. At the fort, they would make any needed repairs to the planes and spend the night. But after flying for only two hours and five minutes they found that they could not continue.[1]

November 12, 1929
Pearce's Diary, airborne to Fort Reliance

In the same aeroplane with the writer were three others of the Dease Point party and they spent most of the time singing, though their voices could hardly be distinguished above the noise of the engine. We passed over hills several hundred feet high and then picked up the Western River and followed it. It is a large stream, and cuts deeply into the country, in places widening into lakes several miles across.

Our course switched to the Backs [Back] River, another large Arctic waterway, and gradually climbed up to the height of land. Our good luck did not hold long. Fog settled down on us near Aylmer Lake, about half way between Burnside and Reliance, and we were forced down on a small lake called Muskox ... The weather was 20 below as we got out of the planes and prepared to stay the night ... There is every evidence of a storm brewing, as the barometer is dropping.

Yet another setback. Weather delays such as this would push the pilots further into the grasp of winter, making flying all the more treacherous or even impossible. The men were keenly disappointed. All hope of completing the first leg of the journey to Fort Reliance was shattered. Stolidly, they accepted their fate and set about making camp and cooking a meal on their Coleman stove. Still in the Barrens with no sheltering forests and thus no timber, they were unable to build any fires to ward off the cold. All they had were their tents and eiderdowns to buffer them from the freezing blasts. Despite cutting snow blocks and piling them around the outside walls of the silk tents to block the wind, it wasn't long before the Arctic temperature crept inside their shelter and prepared to stay there. It would be a long, uncomfortable night.

The storm's rage intensified, and the men spent their time trying to keep warm in their tents as the wind heaped masses of snow against their fragile shelters and their planes. Their body heat combined with the moisture from their breath to form ice on the interior silk walls. When they used the stoves to make tea, the frozen droplets "rained" down on them. There was nothing they could do but wait out the blizzard. For hours snow continued to pile up around the planes and tents. The situation became increasingly tense — they might be immobilized by morning.

To ease the tension, Cruickshank and Semple joked about the necessity to leave the warmth of their tents for a "40 below and

Bill Spence stands beside his shelter at Muskox Lake while. Snow is piled high against the tent in an attempt to keep what warmth could be generated inside and the Arctic blasts out.

a crouch." There were no outhouses or "long drops" at Muskox Lake, which meant taking a shovel, digging a hole in the snow, positioning the shovel for some sort of stability, and then leaning against it. Technique was important in this undertaking, as none of them wished to risk frostbite from coming into contact with the freezing metal, or worse, sticking to it. They attended to their needs with the utmost speed and care. There were no dogs around to help with cleanup. Around that time a story circulated about a newly-enlisted Hudson's Bay manager who, upon arriving at his post in the North, asked his predecessor where the toilets were. The response was a quickly ripped-out page from a catalogue and he was dramatically ushered to the door and shown a snowy landscape with wind blowing in temperatures of -40°C.

Late at night the wind softened and the skies finally cleared. The stars shone in a glittering lacework against the blackness, demonstrating once more the mercurial mood swings of Canada's North. The men drifted to sleep, awakening from time to time throughout the night, shivering with cold despite the body crush inside. Every tent was bulging. Spence's tent alone contained the packed together bodies of Colonel MacAlpine, Colonel Cornwall, Pearce, Blanchet, and Longley.[7]

November 13 dawned with clear skies. Camp was struck early, with the engineers rising before the others in the morning darkness. To their chagrin, they encountered difficulty after difficulty. The snowdrifts caused by the blizzard created an incredible amount of work with the men having to manually dig the planes out of the snow. They worked at a steady pace to keep the sweat from freezing on their bodies. If that did happen, hypothermia would come on twice as fast, and that would be perilous.[3]

During this strenuous workout, Cruickshank made sure each man remained hydrated to keep them warm. Snow had to be melted for this, either over the camp stove or in a canteen kept under their parkas, next to the skin. Eating snow would decrease the core body temperature too quickly and again induce hypothermia and possible shock. At the same time he kept a keen eye on the group for any signs of exposure.

The skis had frozen into the newly fallen snow and the planes had to be manoeuvered from side to side to release them. The men tied ropes to the tails of the planes, the pilots started the engines, and the men laboured in the frigid slipstream, tugging and pulling to try and loosen the skis. Once again, fingers were beyond feeling and their limbs ached from cold, strain, and the cramped, inadequate sleep. Finally, one by one, the planes were released from their icy grip and freed from the drifts. All breathed a sigh of relief when the pilots took their craft on a spin around the lake to polish up the skis. Camp was broken and the men clambered aboard the aircraft.

Hollick-Kenyon suggested that since the air speed indicator on 'SQ was not working, Cruickshank could follow him. When the correct speed for takeoff was reached in the 'SL, Hollick-Kenyon would take to the sky.[4] This suggestion worked, and soon both were airborne. Brown, not far behind, was heading into the Arctic air soon after. The three planes circled above the lake for about half an hour waiting for Bill Spence to take flight.

Once reaching proper speed, Spence eased the aircraft's nose skyward, but as he did so, he hit a hard drift and crashed heavily to the ground. The sound echoed over the flat landscape and the passengers were thrown about the cargo hold. After making sure there were no injuries, the pilot climbed out of his plane to assess the damage. The engine supports were broken and part of the fuselage was damaged.[5] A major blow.

The prospects of repairing Spence's plane, if at all possible, were dismal. Seeing the crash, the first three pilots circled back and landed to discuss the situation. All knew it was vital to take advantage of the good weather and fly out of the Barrens while they had the chance. It was decided that Spence and the mechanics, Tommy Siers and Graham Longley, would stay with 'CZ and do all repairs within their capability. If 'CZ was airworthy, and if they had enough fuel, Spence would then fly the men to Fort Reliance.

If they didn't show up within two days, one of the other pilots would fly back from Reliance with tools, spare parts, and more fuel to assist in the repairs. Siers immediately set about determining what could be done to get 'CZ back into the air, while Spence set up the tent and Longley went out hunting. Siers took out his mechanic's kit and all the equipment they had — from cooking utensils and tools to mess kits — and laid them out in front of him. Whatever they had could potentially be useful. His gift was in being able to visualize each item, not in terms of how it was conventionally used, but in terms of how it *could* be used.

The passengers were redistributed, and the three airworthy planes, now all carrying a heavier load of men, took off into the -30°C sky, heading towards Great Slave Lake and on to Reliance. Cruickshank's "old crock" was holding out under the diligent care of both pilot and mechanic, and 'SQ was carrying far more than the two-passenger limit that Siers had predicted. The increased weight, however, did impact on 'SQ's performance, hampered as it was by the shortened propeller blades and no functioning instruments.

One of their last views of the Barrens was a most amazing sight. It was the caribou. "We had a view of this migration at its flood tide, perhaps never seen before as we saw it from our altitude with

Courtesy of Daryl Goodwin.

The air engineers assess the damage to 'CZ after the second crash into rock-hard drifts.

a fifty mile horizon. The snow was marked by a lace-like pattern, black on white. These were bands of varying numbers in single file, hundreds of thousands — one of the last great migrations of wild-life across a wilderness still comparatively free of their enemies."[6] All were awestruck by the vision from the air.

A few hours later they reached the treeline, something they had not seen in many weeks, and which had a strangely emotional impact on the men. First they spied just a few tiny trees scattered in a white wasteland, and then larger clumps dispersed in the hills, leading to stronger stands of spruce that climbed the hillsides and covered both valley and hilltop. "The sight of trees gave us a genuine feeling of relief."[7] They had made it out of the Barrens and were truly bound for home.

But getting closer to home also brought hazards. Being farther south, Great Slave Lake had not frozen, and the blackness of open water made for some tense moments since all three ski-equipped planes could not land safely unless they found ice. Fog hung low over the lake and visibility was limited. Although the men scanned the landscape below for the Domex base at Fort Reliance, they could not locate it. The pilots did, however, find a landing site at the mouth of the Lockhart River, where the water was shallow and ice had formed. All planes landed without any problems. This put them close to old Fort Reliance, originally built by in 1833 by George Back[8] when he needed a wintering station during an Arctic expedition. The "new" Fort Reliance community, where the Domex base was located, had been built in the vicinity of Back's earlier fort, so actually was nearby.

Tents were set up and soon the sound of axes chopping trees filled the air. Fires were lit and pots of water put on to boil in the surroundings of Back's earlier fort. Only the fireplaces and some other stonework of the old fort remained. Crouching amid the ruins, the men found comfort in the blazing fires and commented how wonderful it was to be in timber again.[9] A sense of security seemed to envelope them. Supper was cooked over the wood fires

Now at the east end of Great Slave Lake, the planes' engines are covered with a canvas "protector" with only the propeller exposed. The men gathered around a campfire to seek what little warmth was available and to cook their food. A large tent was set up on the ice for sleeping quarters.

and tea, flavoured by the low-hanging smoke, was made for all. Cruickshank, however, did not share their sense of well-being — the fact that the pilots were down to three planes was troubling. If by chance they encountered another machine failure, they would be in a challenging situation indeed.

On November 15, several members of the group took their guns to search for game in the cold clear morning air. Before long, shots rang out and the triumphant hunters returned dragging six caribou.[10] Once they had eaten their fill, fuel was transferred to Hollick-Kenyon's 'SL and he took off in search of the Dominion Explorers base at Fort Reliance. The pilot and passengers searched the rocky west shore and finally located it. The inhabitants of the community ran out onto the ice signalling to the pilot that the ice was safe for landing. Hollick-Kenyon, being cautious about the state of the ice, circled above while Blanchet dropped a note saying "Run in a circle if the ice is safe."[11] A small dog caught the note and led the people in a lively chase around the buildings. Snagging the dog at last, the men read the bedraggled note and quickly gave the signal to land. The Domex base had been found.

Courtesy of Daryl Goodwin.

Some of the men sit at the campfire eating a hearty meal at the crumbling remains of George Back's old Fort Reliance. The tent (right) is the typical accommodation for bush pilots.

The men were to be moved over to new Fort Reliance and settled into the base, a site well-stocked with food. As Hollick-Kenyon began to transport a few at a time from the former Back station, 'SL developed engine problems. Upon landing, he also reported that all three planes with full loads would be too much for the relatively thin ice at the Fort Reliance base. It was decided that 'SQ and 'SL would remain at the old fort, and the rest of the group would be transported over by Brown in 'SO. Once 'SO was gassed up from their store of fuel, it taxied along the shoreline to deliver the next contingent to their new quarters, a site with substantial log buildings and manned by the RCMP. After months in the Barrens, Blanchet joked that "This was a metropolis!"[12]

Once again the men had to wait for ice to form. Meanwhile, they were entertained by radio broadcasts about the "lost party" — so recently "found." Since they had not been heard from after leaving Burnside River, and since there was no wireless at Reliance, the media was once again speculating on the missing men and pilots and where they could possibly be. Where were their heroes?

Courtesy of Dary. Goodwin.

Andy Cruickshank, centre, with Roy Brown, far right, and Alf Walker, at left, enjoy a joke as they discuss the events of the past weeks at the old fort.

While sojourning at Fort Reliance, the men tried a spot of curling — Far-North style. Sections of logs were cut into rounds, and into each round a spike was driven to be used as a handle. The wooden rounds were then dipped repeatedly into water and allowed to freeze and refreeze. Once a good solid coating of ice encased the round, a curling "sheet" was cleared, using snow shovels on the ice along the shoreline. Aircraft brooms were used to sweep the ice in front of the wooden "curling stones."[13] Since food and shelter were not a concern, it was time for some fun, and many such games were played during the wait at Reliance. The men also helped with chores, such as building up firewood stocks for winter. In the evenings their drink of choice was a cocktail of wine and gin.

Bill Spence still had not appeared from Muskox Lake. Two days had passed and Cruickshank was concerned about pilot and crew. This could mean one of two things — either they could not make repairs or they had met a further mishap. He wanted to get spare parts to them as soon as possible, so he decided that

Roy Brown, Guy Blanchet, and Paul Davis would set out with supplies on November 16. Accordingly, they packed up the parts and tools needed for Spence's repairs and extra food, including a quarter caribou, but in their haste they forgot to pack the tent. This should not have been a problem, as they fully expected to return to Reliance in the evening, assuming all went well with Spence, Siers, and Longley. A quick turnaround would mean the entire group could begin their final leg no later than November 18, ice permitting.

The sky was clear for the flight, with only a frosty haze. They picked up the Lockhart River with ease on their way to Muskox Lake. Visibility was good for a short time, and then a low cloud forced Brown to fly at only a few hundred feet altitude. Blanchet's comment pointed out the danger of these conditions: "Land and lake were almost indistinguishable."[14] They were only roughly ten miles away from Spence, near Aylmer Lake, yet they could not go on. Brown landed his plane and kept the engine running as they waited for the sky to clear. Once the cloud dissipated, he gathered speed for takeoff. Suddenly, the engine's whine was cut short by a deafening crash and a tremendous impact, jarring pilot and passengers and tossing them like rag dolls. 'SO had hit a hard drift, and the starboard undercarriage collapsed. As the plane swerved and plunged into the snow, ten feet of the fifty-one-foot wooden cantilevered wing crumpled like paper. Nothing short of a new wing and a machine shop would restore 'SO's life.

Meanwhile at Muskox Lake, Tommy Siers and Graham Longley were repairing 'CZ. Siers, as always the innovative and resourceful mechanic, had decided to use the handle of the frying pan to splice the broken component. This worked remarkably well, even by Siers' standards, and he hoped the plane would be airworthy by the following day, November 16. While Siers worked on the plane, Bill Spence built snow walls around their tent to protect them from the freezing winds and prepared the meals.[15] Longley had returned to camp empty-handed and their food stocks were dwindling at a dismaying rate. Unless one of the men had some luck with a gun, they would be out of food within a day or so. Cold and miserable, they kept their ears strained for the sound of a plane coming to assist them.

Just to the south at Aylmer Lake, Brown, Davis, and Blanchet were uninjured but in a state of shock. They had begun the day as the ones bringing assistance to Spence and his crew, and now they were in a very precarious position themselves. They had food, a Coleman stove, and a plumber's pot (the heating torch for the engine and engine oil), but upon checking, they found the only shelter they had was their fabric-covered plane, and it was poised at a very steep angle. Now both Brown and crew at Aylmer Lake and Spence and the mechanics at Muskox Lake were in need of help, and neither could communicate with the group at Reliance or each other. Cruickshank's intuition and sense of foreboding had once again been verified. Two more machine failures had occurred, and Hollick-Kenyon's plane was now no longer airworthy. The trip home was going to prove as difficult and "eventful" as the initial search, possibly even worse.

November 16, 1929
Richard Pearce's Diary, Domex base at Fort Reliance

The weather was fine this morning, and one aeroplane, carrying Brown, Davis and Blanchet, hopped off with food and repair parts for Muskox Lake, where we had left the damaged aeroplane. It is hoped that both machines will be back by night, making an early trip to Stoney Rapids possible. It has been a lazy day, most of the party enjoying themselves indoors reading. Brown didn't get back, so we assumed the plane in the Barrens is still unable to move. Late tonight some of the boys visited the police barracks and heard over the radio that our party was presumed to be at Reliance waiting for favorable weather....

The crews continued to work on Hollick-Kenyon's 'SL and they discovered that the engine had a cracked cylinder. It would need a spare to fly. Since there were no spare cylinders at Reliance, the 'SL was irrevocably grounded. This left only Cruickshank's "old crock" in service, the plane that had been rebuilt after its crash through the ice at Burnside. Siers had shown foresight when he decided 'SQ could be salvaged, as it now rested upon Cruickshank and 'SQ to contend with the airlift back to Winnipeg.

Andy Cruickshank and Alf Walker hiked back to the old fort, where 'SQ and 'SL had remained, and brought 'SQ to the Domex base. The snow was beginning to fall, and there was a need to take action quickly. Cruickshank conferred with Colonel MacAlpine and suggested that he and Walker fly 'SQ to Fort Resolution to request two more relief planes. Colonel MacAlpine agreed, and the mechanics overhauled the "old crock" once again for a long flight to Resolution in the morning.

November 20, 1929
Richard Pearce's Diary, Reliance

Cruickshank got away a little after nine for Resolution. There was no sign of the planes from the Barrens. All of us are worrying about the two parties, for while they have plenty of food to last them some time, it is obvious that unless more is sent soon they will be in distress. We have regular lookouts on the ice, armed with flare pistols, and have brush piles ready to be lighted should a plane be heard. We hope that only weather conditions are holding them up.

At Aylmer Lake, Brown, Blanchet, and Davis were thankful

to be uninjured, but dismayed at the sight that greeted their eyes. Blanchet summed up the men's stunned disbelief: "It seems incredible that the powerful machine which a few moments ago could travel so swiftly through the air, is now helpless"[16] Once over the shock, the three men tried to determine their location. Fortuitously, a cairn that Blanchet had built some years before during a survey expedition was nearby, and from this he knew they were at the end of Five Finger Bay, which happened to be on the route to where Spence and his plane were down.[17] Blanchet hoped that once Cruickshank or Hollick-Kenyon flew to look for Spence, 'SO and her crew would be sighted.

Brown and crew decided to try and walk to Muskox Lake to let Spence know the situation. They soon lost their bearings, and by nightfall had retraced their steps and headed back to 'SO. Upon reaching the plane they set about cooking their evening meal and tried to settle in for the night. The plane, being only fabric-covered, was freezing inside, and the small stove they had did little to warm the cargo-hold area. Sleeping arrangements were also a challenge because of the tilted floor — the men kept sliding about. Concerned about knocking over the stove while they slept, they determined that two would sleep while the third stood watch for two hours at a spell.[18] Whether they needed it or not, literary inspiration was at hand. Blanchet recalled that he "had a copy of Omar Khayyam and we rationed reading it aloud while the light lasted. Its philosophy is enlivening, but such passages as 'a jug of wine and thou' only impressed on us the lack of both. Then would come the time for sleeping (and sliding) and for the night watchman with his cares and his thoughts."[19]

The three men at Muskox Lake couldn't understand why no one had come back to assist them. They were running low on food, and the waiting overshadowed all concerns. Since the repairs to the plane had been completed, they decided to warm the engine. But fuel was extremely low. Their only option was to wait for more to be brought to Muskox Lake before they could attempt the flight to Reliance. With the freezing temperatures, the men warmed their tent with the camp stove. This, however, produced gas fumes, and like Blanchet and Brown, their vision slowly began a painful deterioration. Once the throbbing in their eyes got bad enough, they would open the tent flap and let in the fresh, but frigid air.

Spence was assigned to cook what little food they had remaining, and Siers and Longley attempted to shoot anything on four legs. They were becoming desperate for aid. With the fluctuations in temperature inside the tent, their eiderdowns and clothing had become wet and therefore useless. Wet clothing and bedding are a very dangerous combination in the Arctic, as it is the loft in the feathers that traps pockets of warm air and provides insulation against the cold. Knowing this, and with their mood already dampened, the men were well aware that they faced an unequal struggle against nature. With minimal food or heat, they were on the brink of death.

Meanwhile, as they flew from Reliance to Resolution, Cruickshank and Walker were having trouble of their own.

| TEN |

Two More Planes Down

November 20, 1929
Andy's Diary, airborne to Resolution

*Flew up over clouds. Couldn't get down thru to Resolution
so flew north across Great Slave to Yellowknife [River] and
managed to get down. Distance from Resolution to Yellow
knife over open water [for] 90 miles. Stayed the night and
made very comfortable camp. [I] found it impossible to fly in
fog with no instruments and shall never try that again.*

Mists covering the shoreline had driven Cruickshank off the hills
and over the stormy Great Slave Lake. Skimming over the waves,
his plane entered a fog bank so whitely opaque that it was almost

as if he was flying in a bowl of milk. Cruickshank later wrote in his diary that flying in fog was something that no pilot liked to do since there is no sense of orientation. The pilot can think he is heading left when in fact he is heading right, and he can be gaining or losing altitude without knowing. As a seasoned pilot, Cruickshank remained vigilant in this very dangerous situation.

He was flying blind. Not only was there not enough information for his eyes to process what he was looking at, but he also had no instruments to guide him. With Cruickshank not having any altimeter or turn and bank gauges, Alf Walker was understandably anxious during the flight. As casually as was possible under the circumstances, he remarked, "I don't like this Lindbergh stuff!"[1] Finally, Cruickshank was able to break through the dense whiteness and find a safe place to land 'SQ. After the oil was drained from the engine, they promptly set up camp and put together a warm meal.

Next morning, November 21, they broke camp and got away, landing on a sand bar at Fort Resolution at 2:10 p.m., after another harrowing flight through more thick fog.[2] The sand bar was a piece of luck, since they had no other option when ski-equipped, and this far south of the Arctic Circle there were no frozen lakes for landing. Walker and Cruickshank stayed with Sergeant Clifford of the RCMP and his wife while in Resolution, their stay being extended by bad weather but made pleasant by Mrs. Clifford, who was "wonderfully kind to us and really made us feel at home." However, Cruickshank's thoughts did not rest for long on the comforts of home, as his diary continues, "Must change prop if I go to look for Brown and Spence. Machine has no performance with this cut-off prop. [It] doesn't climb."[3]

Wires were sent to Stony Rapids, but the news that came back was not encouraging. Two planes, one owned by Dominion Explorers and the other by Consolidated Mining and Smelting, had been standing at Stony Rapids during the search and both had sustained damage upon arrival. In a particularly rough landing, pilot Ken Dewar of Consolidated Mining's plane CF-AAM had suffered a structural undercarriage failure, caused by the collapse of the framework supporting the skis and resulting in an aeronautical belly flop. His 'AAM would require some work before it could be declared airworthy again. Meanwhile, pilot Charles Sutton, flying Fairchild CF-AAN had gone through the rubbery ice while landing at Stony Rapids. Once both planes were repaired the pilots would head towards Reliance to assist in the flights to Winnipeg, if needed.

The media in Edmonton and Winnipeg were notified of the situation, and informed readers that Cruickshank was in Resolution requesting replacement planes. He and Walker then waited for the weather to lift so they could return to the Domex base at Fort Reliance.

On November 22, 1929, *The Manitoba Free Press* reported that all members of the Dominion Explorers were safe at Fort Reliance: "Andy Cruickshank, senior Western Canada Airways pilot who has the responsibility for decisions ... [believes] that flight on the homeward bound journey may be confidently essayed ..." This came as welcome news to friends and family of the prospecting group. Several days had elapsed without any communication, and fears were mounting once again that the group was in trouble. In an interview and in the presence of an RCMP officer, Cruickshank reiterated that the MacAlpine party was safe at Reliance after being stranded on the Canadian Barrens by heavy storms and fogs for the past ten days. He continued to describe a very hard trip and adverse flying conditions.

On November 23, Andy Cruickshank and Alf Walker attempted to leave for Fort Reliance where the Domex men were waiting, but they had difficulty taking off due to the deep snow that had fallen during the last few days. Both men had worked into a sweat while clearing the snow, but the heat that warmed their bodies was quickly sucked away by the cold air. Their clothing crackling with frozen sweat, they continued shovelling to get down to the glare ice for the plane to reach maximum takeoff speed. It was a very difficult job. Once the skis were able to slide along the slick, icy runway they had created, 'SQ gathered speed and was soon airborne.

Within minutes, the weather turned into winter. Snowstorms made visibility a nightmare for Cruickshank. For most of the flight he had to fly lower than the height of the hills, along the shore of the vast Great Slave Lake, and over open water again. The forces of nature, nothing if not consistent, conspired against them yet another time: they couldn't make it back to the men at Reliance because of the formidable weather and nor could they carry on with the flight. They decided to make camp about halfway through their journey. It snowed as they slept, and the following morning they had a terrible time getting 'SQ out of the newly formed drifts that had gathered around its base. When they finally reached Fort Reliance on November 24, they discovered that Brown and Spence had still not returned.

A concerned Cruickshank immediately got the black gang overhauling 'SQ for the planned flight back into the Barrens to look for 'SO and 'CZ, but once more he would have to wait on the weather.

Since the snow showed no signs of letting up, dog teams were dispatched with food and messages to Spence, Siers, and Longley. Ten days had elapsed since the crash of 'CZ, and Spence and crew had not made their way to Reliance as planned. This could only mean they were unable to get the plane airworthy, or some other mishap had occurred. The four dog teams were comprised of a trader, who knew the area well, RCMP Corporal Williams, and two teams from the Dominion Explorers. Harnessing the dogs to their sleds was an art and a science. Like humans, sled dogs engage in feuds and so one could not be positioned near an "enemy," or a massive tangle of harnesses and bared teeth would result, requiring time and patience to unravel the lines and pull the fighting canines apart. Despite the risk of chaos, these descendants of wolves were hard-working and intelligent. With final instructions and shouts from their masters, they became a united team, immediately falling silent, leaping at their harnesses as if their lives depended on it, and headed off into the bleak chalky white.

Nearly a week had passed since Roy Brown, Paul Davis, and Guy Blanchet had taken off with spare parts for Spence. Cruickshank had no idea where they were.

———

At Aylmer Lake, Roy Brown and the other two men were struggling to stay alive. They took turns standing "sentry duty" with a flare ready to shoot if they heard the flat drone of a plane, and keeping a vigilant eye on their small gas stove. Daily they waited and hoped that Cruickshank would come to their aid, and daily they were disappointed. Sometimes they thought they heard something, but it just turned out to be the wind or their imagination.

> Days passed from brightness and gleaming white into shades of twilight, deepening into night. There was disappointment but we did not speak of the — tomorrow — perhaps Andy's crock — something might have happened at the base…. The North teaches patience, not perhaps in little things, but the patience of the Spirit that must meet the moods of nature through the long seasons and in the surrounding vast wilderness."[4]

In the face of freezing temperatures and high winds, it was essential to stay indoors as much as possible, but without their gas stove they would have frozen to death. Unfortunately, serious problems developed as a result. As Spence and his crew had also experienced, the fumes from the stove almost caused Blanchet, Davis, and Brown to go blind. Pain in their eyes signalled the need to clear the air, and they had to keep opening the door of 'SO, which resulted in heat loss. It became a vicious cycle. They could not stay warm without risking vision loss, but to save their eyesight they had to risk freezing to death.

At one point Blanchet nearly set the plane — a flimsy construction of fabric and gasoline tanks — into a raging inferno when some coals fell out of his pipe and landed on the upholstery of the seat. Once the smoke came to Blanchet's attention, he grabbed the seat and threw it out of the door. The wind then whipped up the flames into a fireball, fortunately away from the plane.[5]

The three discussed the possible reasons why no plane had come looking for them. They were a mere three hours' flying time away from Fort Reliance, and although weather had been bad, they still felt a flight could have made it through. No matter what the topic of discussion, food was never far from their thoughts. They were always hungry. Their food supplies were dismal, their emergency ration box had been pillaged from previous flights, and they were reduced to boiling caribou bones several times for its meagre nourishment.

Paul Davis, Brown's mechanic, tried to make light of their situation. He chose the small cup and spoon from their kit, saying eating with the small utensils made his rations seem larger, and that made him think of Goldilocks and the Three Bears. They discussed anything and everything — wine and women, as often as not — trying to avoid silence, which led to thinking and worry. Enlarging on the theme of women, one night Roy Brown commented, "When I get home, I expect that I'll meet my daughter [aged six weeks when he left] coming home from school."[6] Davis did not respond to this story — "girls of six weeks did not interest him."[7] He seemed to be a man of some experience, complaining to Brown one night that "he had never slept with anyone who had so many elbows and knees."[8]

On the 23rd, they decided to make a move and try to walk out. Paul Davis took a ski off 'SO and used their tarp to make a kind of toboggan. Towing the awkward contraption was arduous work for these hunger-weakened men as they trudged into the face of the raw, fierce Arctic snowstorm. Keeping their faces parallel to the ground to avoid the sting of the airborne ice crystals strained their backs even more. After only twelve miles they settled in for the night, on the ski, under the tarp. They cooked a meal, and the steam from the stove rose to the roof of the tarp and formed condensation, which froze. When the temperature rose inside their makeshift tent because of body heat, the frost melted, showering the men, who then, like Spence, Siers, and Longley at Muskox Lake, now had wet eiderdowns and clothing. Wisely, they made the decision to return to their plane the following morning to wait for either Cruickshank or Hollick-Kenyon to come to their aid. They did not speak of waiting for death.

During this time 'SQ was being readied for its return to the Barrens. The black gang had given the plane a ten-hour overhaul, but still it failed to achieve airworthy inspection. Cruickshank decided that the only way he could fly would be to temporarily borrow the spare parts of Hollick-Kenyon's grounded plane. He asked Walker to take the propeller from 'SL so 'SQ could reach maximum power when it flew back to the Barrens, and he also had the engineers install the tachometer and the altimeter from 'SL. On November 26, eleven days after leaving 'CZ at Muskox Lake, 'SQ headed back into the Barrens to bring fuel and food to Spence, and to look for Brown and crew of 'SO. That day, Andy Cruickshank recorded the events in his diary: "Took off for Muskox with two drums of gas and 400 lbs of rations at 8:15. Landed [at] Aylmer Lake. Found Brown's machine apparently crashed and at first sight saw no signs of occupation and got really nervous. After one circle party ran out of machine and [I] was greatly relieved."

It had started as just another day of waiting for Brown and his crew but during breakfast they heard a faint hum. None of the men said a word, each just thinking it was his imagination, but the hum became progressively louder. Scrambling out of 'SO, Guy Blanchet lit the flare. Paul Davis hollered above the noise, "Good old Andy's crock!" Cruickshank wig-wagged 'SQ's wings and made a search for a safe place to land. Blanchet, Brown, and Davis were never so glad to see anyone in their lives. Cruickshank said he had sighted the wreck miles away and did not expect to find anyone alive. When he saw the men running about, his "Poor devils!" changed to "I'll be damned!" — expressing sincere sympathy and real pleasure.[9]

Cruickshank filled them in on the news from Fort Reliance and said that since Spence had not returned, and Hollick-Kenyon's 'SL had developed a cracked cylinder, he and Walker had flown to Resolution and arranged for two relief planes to fly up from Stony Rapids to assist in the evacuation. He told them there was a genuine worry from the Domex men about ever reaching home, as it seemed each time a plane took off it did not return. Walker chimed in, explaining how their one-day flight to Resolution had turned into three, and then told of missing 'CZ and 'SO, adding to the anxiety that was felt. It appeared that the bad luck that had started with the sinking of the Fokker Super Universal in Churchill Harbour in late August was continuing to plague the group.

The men agreed that Cruickshank should head to Bill Spence and the men at Muskox Lake, where, he hoped, Siers and Longley had been able to repair 'CZ. He would then return for Blanchet, Brown, and Davis. Since days had passed, Cruickshank was concerned they must be out of food, unless one of the men had been successful with a gun. He and Walker readied 'SQ for the flight but unfortunately 'SQ developed a sticky valve, and then burst an oil line.[10] As daylight ebbed, there was no choice but to stay. The five men spent a very cramped night together in Cruickshank's tent. At least on this night they had food and new topics of conversation.

By now, Spence, Siers, and Longley, still marooned at Muskox Lake, were in desperate need of help. They could not understand why no one had come back for them. They had run out of food, but during the night of November 26, an unlucky fox wandered too close to camp, and Siers managed to shoot it. They cooked up an Arctic fox stew with the last handful of beans, which gave them some sustenance. However, their clothes and eiderdowns were still wet, and, since they had no means of making a fire to dry anything, they stayed together inside the tent, wet, freezing, and disheartened. The temperature was -45°C, cold enough to freeze the ink in Spence's pen while writing his diary,[11] as well as the last remaining rum ration in the bottle! Any optimism they possessed had quickly dissipated in the metallic-smelling Arctic air.

For thirteen days they had had little to do but hope and wait, and as they waited they picked out a good place for a relief plane to land, if one was to come. As the days passed they became increasingly depressed and concerned about the other planes and felt sure there had been a serious mishap.[12] Bill Spence began each diary entry with a weather report and hopes that a plane was forthcoming, and ended with the observation that a plane had not come and they were "very blue" when none arrived. They waited.

And still nothing.

———

At Fort Reliance, Pearce, too, was keeping his daily log:

November 21, 1929
Pearce's Diary, Fort Reliance

There are still no aeroplanes, though we had hoped that at least Cruickshank's would return from Muskox Lake, as the weather was fairly good. We also thought there was a good chance of Sutton and another aeroplane coming through from Stoney [*sic*] Rapids. A steady watch was kept up through the daylight hours, from about 9:30 to 3:30. With a fair wind blowing it was a little chilly standing around on the lake.

Uncertainty permeated everyone's thoughts at Reliance. They just couldn't believe that each time a plane took off, it did not return as expected. The only remaining plane at Reliance was Hollick-Kenyon's 'SL, and it was out of commission with the cracked cylinder. The day dragged. To keep themselves somewhat entertained they continued to curl, play darts and read. And they waited.

Alf Walker awoke at Aylmer Lake well before what daylight could be expected, and started the ritual of getting the plane ready for flight. After a quick breakfast, Cruickshank and Walker warmed up 'SQ. They told Brown that they would return the same day after giving Spence assistance. Then the plan was that Cruickshank would return to pick up Brown and crew and they would head to Fort Reliance. After a safe takeoff, Cruickshank headed towards Muskox Lake and the 'CZ. Brown watched 'SQ fly towards Spence. Then the men at Aylmer Lake waited for Cruickshank to return.

November 27, 1929.
Andy's Diary, Muskox Lake,

Took off to look for Spence's machine. Found the party and machine. Party been on very short rations, living on fox meat. All suffering from blindness owing to gas fumes. Must have been very cold and uncomfortable. Got Spence's engine running but she was missing badly. Started SQ again and had oil line burst for the second time. Spent [a] miserable night in the cold. Noticed Spence, Siers and Longley's clothing and bedding all wet. Guess we were just in time....

A person loses just over half a litre of moisture in sweat a night, and this moisture can quickly build up inside the eiderdown, limiting the insulation properties of the covering. Wet cloth or bedding can cause hypothermia, leading to death. Cruickshank and Walker did their best to warm up the cold men, and, with the provisions they brought, prepared a most welcome hearty meal.

The following morning, November 28, the mechanics got both 'CZ and 'SQ ready for flying. Once airworthiness was passed, the planes would head back to Brown and crew, pick them up and then fly on to Fort Reliance. Despite the importance of their careful planning, actual outcomes were out of their control. Spence had difficulty taking off, and he crashed 'CZ into a snowdrift, damaging the fuselage. The repairs made by Siers and Longely, including the innovation with the frying pan handle had all withstood the crash, but with the damage to the fuselage, 'CZ, originally called the *City of New York*, came to rest far from its urban namesake. It was abandoned and the three men climbed aboard 'SQ with Cruickshank and Walker. The "old crock" took off safely, and her pilot headed towards Aylmer Lake.

Brown, Blanchet, and Davis had been concerned when Cruickshank had not returned the same day he left. Blanchet wrote, "We were in the mood to expect some new disaster. To reduce pessimism to absurdity, I suggested that Andy [Cruickshank] would return next day with Bill's [Spence] party and pick us up and set out for Reliance. Meanwhile Ken [Hollick-Kenyon] would have been dispatched to see what was the trouble. The two planes would meet in a head-on collision and, crashing to earth, would fall on the dogs."[13]

Brown and crew had stayed in their plane and waited for the men that would rescue them. They were bereft of all energy and initiative and stared wordlessly as 'SQ finally circled above them. Cruickshank landed, and he kept the engine running while the three men crammed themselves into the cabin area with their gear. Just before he took off, he and Walker took a cylinder from 'SO to replace the cracked part on Hollick-Kenyon's 'SL. This was in the hopes that 'SL could be repaired and used for the flight home. When they took to the air, there were eight men, with gear, in the reworked 'SQ. Walker had had to use his bootlace to tie the door shut. When Blanchet asked if this was safe, Walker replied, "Oh yes, if Andy doesn't bank."[14] Blanchet pictured a sudden manoeuvre in the air, with oilcans, wrenches, and people spilling out of 'SQ onto the Barrens below.[15]

On November 28, during the flight back, the sun was shining and the hills of the Barrens gave way to the timber stands near Fort Reliance. Cruickshank had managed to bring everyone safely back to the waiting Domex group — a nerve-wracking flight for him and one that brought great relief when he reached Reliance.[16] There, the tales were told. Both Spence and his crew and Brown and his crew had harrowing stories to relate, but both groups expressed their gratitude to Cruickshank for getting them safely out. Typically, Cruickshank brushed these off. Everyone was relieved that the group was safe and together once more.

Later that night, a Native runner brought in word that one of the four dog teams was returning. RCMP Corporal Williams had cut his foot with an axe, and there was concern that frostbite would occur on the open wound. When Williams pulled in with his team, Doctor Bruce tended to the injury immediately. The three other dog teams had continued on their journey, not knowing that Cruickshank had brought the stranded men back to Reliance. Soon enough, however, the dog teams would find the abandoned planes and return to Reliance. It had been proposed that a plane be sent out to the dog teams, but Corporal Williams said he did not feel that was necessary.

Cruickshank went outside to check his plane for the flight the next morning. He was now filled with a sense of relief and he was certain all was going to end well — his sixth sense, always reliable, told him so. His plane was flying as well as could be expected, 'SL's cylinder had been replaced, and 'AAN, and 'AAM would be leaving Stony Rapids to assist in the evacuation as soon as they were airworthy.

Eleven

A Crowded Journey Home

Pearce's Diary, Fort Reliance
December 2, 1929

Doc. Bruce is anxious to get Don. Goodwin out, as he will have to amputate some toes. Cruickshanks' old S.Q. will take out Brown, Goodwin, Doc. Bruce, Alf Walker and myself. Colonel MacAlpine says he'll stay at Stony Rapids until the boys are out from [Fort] Reliance.

From here on out, the rescue operation became a taxi service, ferrying groups of men, by stages, toward Winnipeg. After discussions, the southbound route was agreed upon and the men were divided between the two serviceable planes. Andy

Cruickshank and Bertie Hollick-Kenyon would be the advance guard, with Charles Sutton and Ken Dewar flying the next group out once they arrived in Reliance. All the working instruments had been returned to Hollick-Kenyon's 'SL, and Cruickshank was left again to "fly blind." For one last time the men had to clear a runway for the planes to safely taxi.

At least twelve inches of loose, powdery snow needed clearing, down to glare ice.[1] Men worked like Sisyphus, shovelling away the fluffy stuff and watching it settle back on the icy glaze and pushing it off again, slipping and sliding as they went. Meanwhile, the mechanics heated the engines. Great quantities of fog rose into the surrounding air from this process, and since the day was windless, the air became thick with the gassy odour of moisture vapor. It would be a difficult takeoff.

After the runway was completely clear, the men said their goodbyes. Emotions may have been in turmoil, but were held in check as they merely shook their hosts' hands and waved cheerily as they boarded the planes. At 8:00 a.m. the advance guard, led by Cruickshank and Hollick-Kenyon, were ready for the first leg south. Colonel MacAlpine, Guy Blanchet, Brodie Boadway, Stan MacMillan, Don Goodwin, Doc Bruce, Richard Pearce, Bill Nadin, and Alf Walker were in this group. Those remaining were eager to leave Fort Reliance, but showed no signs of regret; they had no choice but to wait for pilots Dewar and Sutton to return for them. The course all pilots would follow was set for Stony Rapids, The Pas, Cranberry Portage, and finally Winnipeg.

Cruickshank was the first to taxi for takeoff. 'SQ stirred up a dense cloud of snow, higher than the plane's windows, which mixed with the fog vapour from the engines exhaust, rendering visibility almost zero. Familiar with the terrain at Fort Reliance, he knew there were obstacles such as trees and buildings to avoid. In these conditions he could only hope that he was on the right track. Feeling the airplane moving forward and the power of the engine, and listening intently to the sound of the engine indicating takeoff speed had been reached, he gently pulled back on the stick and lifted off into the air. He breathed a sigh of relief when he exited the fog and snow cloud and headed into a clear sky. Hollick-Kenyon was right behind him.

It was a smooth trip in the beginning, but then the air became turbulent as they headed east towards Stony Rapids. Blanchet was certain of their flight path, but Cruickshank disagreed with him. After some heated discussion, Cruickshank landed the plane on a small lake near the Slave River, and again Hollick-Kenyon followed him. They conferred and agreed that Cruickshank's route out was indeed the correct one and he would continue to be in charge of their flight plan.

The small lake they had landed on was covered by a foot of more loose snow, which had to be cleared before they could resume their flight south. Once again this was done, and once again clouds of powdery snow obscured vision as the pilots coaxed their planes into the air. Cruickshank had a difficult time getting sufficient speed for takeoff, but once airborne, followed the route he knew, and the planes were back on course.[2] This route took them over Lake Athabasca, which had still not frozen, and rising air currents caused more turbulence. Flying over open water made both Cruickshank and Hollick-Kenyon uneasy, but it wasn't long before they found ice at the narrow end of the lake near their destination. The worthy inhabitants of Stony Rapids had received word through their wireless that their community was on the homeward-bound route and had written "LAND HERE" in the snow. The two pilots lined up and glided in safely.[3]

To say there was rejoicing would be an understatement. The people at Stony Rapids gave the men a rousing welcome, and many willing hands assisted with the planes. Besieged with requests to tell the tale, the exhausted men obliged. Soon food was served up, and the evening conversation continued to centre on the Dominion Explorers expedition and the efforts by the search teams. It was then, while telling the combined stories of the search team and the stranded men that the realization of their remarkable good fortune truly hit home.

Within the safety and warmth of the tiny community of Stony Rapids the men had no need to look beyond their log cabin walls. But beyond this dot on the landscape, the bigger economic picture was grim. The news of the Canadian economy was bad, and all knew that the repercussions were serious. Voices were hushed as stories of terrible losses and suicides were recounted. Yet to the rescuers and the rescued, this news seemed far less life-changing than what they had just gone through. In the vast wilderness of the North, news of the Outside could not really touch them. They did not look at the future. They focused only on getting home.

Colonel MacAlpine excused himself and left the gathering for the wireless station, where he began sending off wires to the Dominion Explorers headquarters and to all the families to give the update on the eighteen days' silence since leaving Bathurst. He also wired Jim Vance and Blasdale at Baker Lake. Cruickshank had received orders that no Western Canada Airways planes were to fly into Baker Lake at this time of year to assist Vance, and, in fact, the three WCA planes were to fly to Winnipeg immediately.

MacAlpine, however, was adamant that he send help to Vance, as both Blasdale and Vance had risked their lives for those of the Dominion Explorers. He did not want to desert the pilot and mechanic who had worked so tirelessly in the rescue effort. He worked out a plan to retrieve the two men. Bill Spence volunteered to fly the Dominion Explorer plane 'AAN back to Baker Lake once the evacuation was complete. He would fly from Winnipeg, via Hudson Bay to Baker Lake, with the tail assembly for Vance, and then Vance would fly 'RK back to Winnipeg with Blasdale. Domex in Toronto, however, vetoed this decision, as did Vance. His wire read back to MacAlpine read: "Suggest you reconsider matter on purely business basis disregarding personal aspect STOP We will cheerfully go out on foot."

MacAlpine responded:

> Reference your wire Toronto apparently concurring views from Winnipeg and have no doubt when I get Toronto could have same reversed but there is no time to do that and get to Baker and back in time for reasonable flying STOP Your willingness to abandon the personal side takes away only alibi for defending my action STOP Your telegram shows broad gauge caliber and I have no alternative but to agree STOP Hope you have a good trip out and be sure to see me Toronto.

It was a night filled with anticipation. Stony Rapids was one stop closer to Winnipeg. Wires were coming in and so was more news, this time of the gloomy financial state of Dominion Explorers. Although the economic outlook was bleak, relief and excitement over returning home continued to overshadow the news. The evening sky at Stony was filled with billions of stars and the pulsating aurora borealis. The solar wind spun and whipped greens, iridescent blues, oranges, and pinks across the backdrop of a velvety black night. Cruickshank stood outside and watched this display with a sense of peace. He could never get enough of this immense country that he respected and admired. The North was the genesis for the adventurous life he had embarked upon, and the wings of a plane had taken him closest to what he was seeking.

He walked around his "old crock," climbed into the cockpit, and reviewed the series of events that could have led to an unthinkable outcome. Minor and not so minor mistakes could have added up to dire consequences. But the unlucky events were simply that — unlucky, not catastrophic. Both the Domex men and the search and rescue teams had survived the perils of a savage Arctic winter in one of the most remote regions on earth, where they were battered by storms of the fiercest magnitude. They had survived isolation, starvation, privation, plane crashes, and freezing temperatures. Cruickshank believed that central to all successful outcomes must be a shared goal. These individuals did have a common goal, and, working together they became worthy adversaries of the forces of nature.

Cruickshank went back inside to discuss the route out for the following day. He would continue to fly the advance guard, and along with him in 'SQ would be Alf Walker, Roy Brown, Dr. Don Bruce, Richard Pearce, and Don Goodwin. Dr. Bruce had been in contact with the hospital in The Pas and had arranged for Goodwin's surgery. The men eventually settled down for the night, this nighttime in warmth and comfort.

December 1 was not fit for flying, so the mechanics spent the day servicing the aircraft. Richard Pearce decided to take some time and visit the nearby Dominion Explorers' Axis Lake project where they were drilling for diamonds. Dominion Explorers had staked a claim here based on copper and nickel finds, but had found diamonds in the core samples. It was roughly an eight-mile walk from Stony Rapids, and being a mining man, Pearce couldn't help but do some "on site ground work" for the newspaper while he was there. He had an enjoyable day visiting friends and checking out the progress of the exploration site. As the future would show, the North Athabasca Basin, where the Domex men were prospecting, would be cause for excitement.

Upon his return to Stony Rapids, Pearce and some of the other men paid a visit to Corporal Stallworthy of the RCMP. Cruickshank and Stalsworthy had many a tale to tell of their patrols in the Arctic, and the listeners were captivated. It was a special breed of officer who filled an RCMP post in the northern "wastes" of Canada — a man who was resourceful, tough, and resilient and who had a sense of humour. These qualities emerged in their storytelling.

Cruickshank related a humorous tale of dog-sled racing while in Dawson, Yukon Territory. He bred his own dogs and trained them in the harness. Bruce, his young lead dog, was more wolf than dog and "not a very affectionate fellow, but hard working and intelligent." The RCMP had bought the team from Cruickshank, and it was with this team he did his Arctic patrols and entered a Dog Derby, not unlike the modern day Iditarod.[4]

The race in 1926 was an intense one through the rugged terrain of the Yukon Territory. From the beginning, Cruickshank and his dogs were in the lead. On the home stretch, crowds lined the snow-packed trail leading into Dawson. Their enthusiastic shouts filled the air as each team and their driver hit the final leg. The race route took Cruickshank right past his house, where one of his other dogs decided to charge out and join in the fun. Within seconds, Cruickshank's team became a tangled mass of fur and leather, with barking dogs and wagging tails, and he lost forty seconds trying to untangle the noisy heap. Once back on the trail Cruickshank was still in the lead, but the cheering crowd converged and blocked the road at the finish line. Cruickshank's leader panicked and pulled him and the rest of the team into a very deep snow pile. All ended up in a mass of fur, shouts, and barks, and Cruickshank lost another minute as he tried to drag the whole bunch of dogs and overturned sled over the finish line. He came in only third, but was nonetheless proud of his team.[5]

This was a very busy day, with wires continually coming in. One gave the news from Resolution that pilots Sutton and Dewar had left the fort and were heading towards Fort Reliance to pick up the remainder of the group. This was encouraging, as it meant that soon all the men would be on their way back to Winnipeg. The evening was dedicated to good times, with icicle-chilled drinks, card games and, of course, more stories.

The weather on December 2, began as fair, and passengers Goodwin, Pearce, Doc Bruce, and Brown piled into 'SQ with engineer Walker and pilot Cruickshank. He would be flying solo for this leg of the journey to The Pas, where Goodwin was to receive surgery. Cruickshank was concentrating on delivering his injured passenger in the quickest time possible. But it wasn't long before trouble arose. His diary entry for December 2, 1929, en route to The Pas noted: "Visibility [was] rotten some of the way. Had to land twice and wait for snowstorms. Arrived Cranberry after dark. Spent night in Roy Brown's cabin."

It was 4:30 in late afternoon when 'SQ landed for the third time. This time the group would not continue on to their destination at The Pas. Goodwin was carried out of the plane into the cabin. A fire was lit in the stove and they made the best of the evening and just hoped that the next morning, December 3, would bring more desirable weather.

After 'SQ flew out of Stony Rapids on December 2, Colonel MacAlpine, Stan McMillan, Brodie Boadway, Guy Blanchet, Bill Nadin, and Herbert Hollick-Kenyon were making their own plans to leave. Tommy Thompson, Alex Milne, and Major Robert Baker were still, it was thought, at Reliance with the others who were waiting to catch the flight back to Winnipeg with pilots Dewar and Sutton. It would be a scattered welcome home party, with media coverage in turmoil as to where to go. Some representatives of the press had gone to Churchill to cover the story, a location where none of the pilots had landed. Once they received the message from Stony Rapids that Cranberry Portage and The Pas were the touch-down locations for refuelling, the press once again hared off to meet the men.[6]

Before 'SL took off from Stony Rapids, a message was received on the wireless and conveyed to MacAlpine. Dewar and Sutton had arrived at Reliance to pick up the last group of men and were en route back to Stony Rapids. It had taken the pilots an adventurous three days to travel the three hundred miles from Stony. They had arrived at Reliance in a driving blizzard.[7] Both pilots had trouble finding the base in the snowstorm, but after some time had managed to do so. Sutton's plane partially broke through the ice upon landing, but the men manoeuvred it back on firm ice before any damage was done. The final group, including the Dominion Explorers men Major Baker, Alex Milne, and Tommy Thompson, were loaded aboard 'AAN and 'AAM, and the pilots took off on their return journey to Stony Rapids. MacAlpine had been waiting there for their arrival, and once the planes had refuelled all would continue to Cranberry Portage and then The Pas. By now Cruickshank and his passengers had already arrived in The Pas.

The front page of *The Manitoba Free Press*, December 4, 1929, ran this story:

> Out of a grey sky a yellow and blue Fokker today brought the first part of the MacAlpine party to The Pas, the first large centre since they left civilization several months past.
>
> The plane landed on Halcrow Lake here, and immediately a rush of taxis carried leading citizens and close friends of a number of the passengers on the plane to the spot where they landed. All of the party, consisting of Andy Cruikshank [*sic*], Roy Brown, Dr D.L. Bruce, A. Walker, Richard Pearce, got out except for Donald Goodwin, mechanic, whose feet were frozen. The party carried Goodwin to the taxis, and asked him if he should be taken to the hospital, but he declared, "I am going to have some fun before they operate on me."

It is not recorded how Goodwin spent that evening but it is likely that a hot bath, drinks with friends, and a good night's sleep on a fresh mattress figured into his plans. After his "evening of fun," Goodwin was driven to St Anthony's Hospital in downtown The Pas for surgery. Astounding as it may seem, despite crashes into barely frozen lakes, sustaining extensive aircraft damage, collapsing shelters, near-starvation, and many miles of trekking over barely frozen ice, dodging open leads, and climbing ice hummocks, the most serious injury was Goodwin's two frostbitten toes.

At the press rally later that day, Roy Brown, always the popular commercial aviator, was asked by dozens of his friends to tell them the story of the great search, but Brown declared it was all over and he wanted to forget it as much as possible. This was a common statement from all the men involved, but the media wouldn't let up and clamoured for details. Cruickshank felt that since he was in charge, he should give a report to the press. He began by assuring the rabid newshounds that, "We were never really starving, but at one time we only had 12 bad herrings amongst the entire crowd."

The group travelled by taxi to another group of reporters at another hotel. By this time the "heroes" thought it best to give in to the journalists' demands, and, once all had gathered, the men demonstrated an "Eskimo song" taught to them at Fort Reliance for the newspapermen. The lively interview continued and more details emerged. If the men came out of their experience in the Barrens with a bit of cultural knowledge, they also left something behind, or, as Richard Pearce jokingly commented, "We have left planes scattered over the North. One we lost in the tide at Churchill. Two are pulled up on the shore near Dease Point in Queen Maud Gulf, in the Arctic sea. One lies wrecked on Muskox Lake: another on Aylmer Lake, with a wing gone. One machine remains at Baker Lake, housed for the winter … We have travelled far and seen much, but nothing as pleasing as the railway tracks at Cranberry Portage." This story was relayed to Pearce's own newspaper, *The Northern Miner*, on December 5, 1929. Perhaps because he had had enough of planes, he decided to board the train and head on to Winnipeg by rail.

—————

Back at Stony Rapids, on December 3, Hollick-Kenyon advanced on the throttle and 'SL climbed with its passengers into the frosty air. They had had to wait for the mist that was rising from nearby rapids to blow away, but once the sky was clear they had no problem in following the predetermined route. Pilots Dewar and Sutton were right behind them.

'SL flew over Reindeer Lake and crossed over the Churchill River near Island Falls, the site of Flin Flon's power plant. Then Cranberry Portage came into sight, and Hollick-Kenyon landed to refuel. The press met them, and again there was a rush of photos taken and stories told, but the pilot was keen to get back into the air and fly onward, so he scooped up his passengers and spirited them away again to the next stop. Darkness had fallen by then. In the distance the pilot and his air engineer saw the lights of The Pas. Beyond the lights was the frozen lake, and 'SL circled above the landing area, gradually losing altitude. Within minutes of Hollick-Kenyon's landing, taxis pulled up alongside the plane and whisked the passengers into the lights and crowd of a hotel where they would spend the night.[8] Colonel MacAlpine was left behind at Cranberry Portage with Captain Sutton, Bill Spence, Alex Milne, Robert Baker, and J.C. Rogers, (a passenger from Stony Rapids), awaiting the arrival of pilot Ken Dewar the following day.

First thing the following morning, Hollick-Kenyon, Blanchet, Nadin, Longley, Davis, MacMillan, and Boadway boarded the 'SL and flew directly to Winnipeg. *The Manitoba Free Press* on December 6, 1929, recapped the story:

Just as dusk began to fall today plane GCXL [*sic* G-CASL], piloted by Captain Hollick-Kenyon, the second contingent of the MacAlpine Party, and its rescuers, slid to a standstill at the Western Canada Airways' dock on the Athabaskow [Cranberry Portage] to be followed fifteen minutes later by a second machine piloted by Captain Sutton. Carrying the third contingent still another plane remains to come and as it was apparently taking off at Stony Rapids when the first two took the air at noon today, it was presumed to be close behind.

As the minutes went by, however, pilots of the first two machines came to the conclusion that as Dewar, piloting the third machine, would know he could scarcely make a landing at Cranberry before dark, he probably is spending the night at Southend, 250 miles northwest of this point, and will likely arrive quite early Friday morning.

Cruickshank, Walker, and Brown had already left The Pas and on December 5 after the safe delivery of Goodwin and Dr. Bruce, the Fokker Super Universal landed at Western Canada Airways Brandon Avenue Airdrome, Winnipeg, shortly before 3:00 p.m.

The Airdrome situated at the end of Brandon Avenue along the Red River, was a bustling hub of aviation activity. It was an air harbour, equipped with seaplane anchorage, and had a small field for takeoff and landing on wheels. It was also Western Canada Airways' major overhaul and repair centre. The Airdrome consisted of separate buildings, housing offices, stores, a wing and fuselage repair shop, and test stands for running the engines. Planes could take off and land on floats during open water season and on skis during the months when the river was frozen. Cruickshank had made the flight to Brandon Avenue in a record time of three hours, flying through fine weather conditions and landing on the frozen Red River. After receiving a warm welcome from the staff at WCA, Cruickshank, Walker, and Brown headed to the Fort Garry Hotel where they were once again interviewed by the press.

Roy Brown tried to slough off the words "epic" and "heroic." He said that if anyone was heroic, it was the mechanics. Both Brown and Cruickshank expounded on the feats of the air engineers, who were by then known as "The Royal and Disorderly Order of the Black Gang." The pilots said that these men had taken the hard knocks of the venture, and described them as "superhuman." They named each air engineer individually: Tommy Siers, in charge of the mechanics, Paul Davis, Graham Longley, Bill Nadin, Pat Semple, and Alf Walker. Brown put it simply: "The fact the airplanes came back is due to them."[9] Cruickshank agreed, commenting laconically to the reporter from the *The Manitoba Free Press* on December 6, 1929, that he just could not say enough about them. Both pilots gave details of their northern search and rescue to yet another group of reporters from the newspaper that same day:

> Flying without many of the necessary instruments and with shortened propeller blades for 1,500 miles in 4 long hops, was one of the feats of Andy Cruickshank, WCA pilot who was in charge of the air squadron searching for the missing MacAlpine party and responsible for seeing them safely brought out from Canada's Arctic wastes. This was disclosed during the course of a brief interview with the intrepid airman at the Fort Garry Hotel last night, when he appeared willing to discuss anything but what he had done himself in the North.

True to form, Cruickshank kept his own counsel on his participation. As an ex-RCMP he was more than willing to tell the facts, but he did so without embellishment. His goal was to return to his little house in Prince George and his family as quickly as possible. Once he finished with the interviews he was driven to WCA head office at Brandon Avenue to fill out a pilot report. He did this with the thoroughness that he was known for, even though he was keen to take to the skies and head home. He had not seen his family for eighty-two days.

As Cruickshank filled out his reports, the events of the past few months flooded back quickly. He referred to his diary constantly and was amazed when he added up his mileage. He had flown over 7,000 miles on the search. This mileage would ultimately be determined to be the most miles flown by any of the search pilots, and many of those miles had been flown without the assistance of his instrument panel. He had fulfilled the order from Leigh Brintnell, and all the men and planes in his charge were safely back "Outside." It was unfortunate that Jim Vance and B.C. Blasdale had to take a dog team from Baker Lake to Churchill, but Cruickshank had done everything within his power to bring assistance back to Vance. Ever the businessman, Brintnell had made the decision that the Western Canada Airways planes must come out, and the Dominion Explorers headquarters had said the same about their own planes, which then left Vance and Blasdale from Northern Aerial Mineral Exploration to find their own way home. Of all the events that had occurred, this was one that Cruickshank wished he could have changed.

By December 7, 'SL, 'AAN, and 'AAM had returned safely to Winnipeg. Cruickshank was not there to greet them since he had returned to Esmé and Dawn. Waiting for the arrival of 'AAN was Roderick MacAlpine, the colonel's twenty-year-old son. As his father climbed out of the plane, Roderick, who had travelled from Toronto, was there to welcome him with open arms. It had been months of waiting, months of worry

The dramatic air hunt comes to a close with the last of the Dominion Explorers being welcomed in Winnipeg by a group of well wishers and reporters. During the search, newspapers carried almost daily stories of the search for the eight missing men.

and strain. MacAlpine's mother had been interviewed by *The Manitoba Free Press* on November 5, 1929. She was reported as saying, "I just can't talk, I just can't. It's been such a terrible strain and I'm sorry. I'm not very strong just now. Oh, I'm so thankful that my son and all of his brave companions have been found alive and well.... I don't know why, for there was certainly little enough encouragement but I had believed most of the time that they would be found again all right ... It's wonderful. It's tremendous."[10]

It was not such a happy homecoming for Alex Milne. Just a few days prior to Milne's arrival home, his widowed mother had passed away. *The Manitoba Free Press* on December 3, 1929, gave details that Milne's mother, Helen, had died after a very short illness, and although she was not present to welcome her son home, she did know that Milne was safe, and was in the process of returning to Winnipeg.

Cupid, however, did bring happiness for two other air engineers. The nuptials that were postponed during the search were once again being planned. Graham Longley, with his bride-to-be Irene Kensington, was due to set sail for England on their honeymoon the day Longley arrived back in Winnipeg. In a stroke of good fortune, *The Manitoba Free Press*, in its December 7, 1929, edition printed that the SS *Duchess of Richmond* would depart on December 14, and there was space for the happy soon-to-be newlyweds. Bill Nadin and his fiancée would be married as soon as their plans could be put back in place.[11]

The wife of Stanley MacMillan summed it up best when she commented on the notion of the brave women behind the adventurous men. A reporter from *The Manitoba Free Press* on December 7, 1929, remarked that now her troubles were over, and she calmly replied, "Yes, for this time at any rate…. for men must work and women must weep." But for now, this was journey's end.

———

Eighty-two days earlier, Lieutenant Colonel Cyril MacAlpine had flown out in search of mineral resources that would, he thought, propel Canada into the status of a civilized and great nation. He found no gold, silver, or diamonds on this journey but something else instead, something of far greater value, in fact a means to this end. Throughout the months he was stranded high above the Arctic Circle, his life took on a different perspective. As the men struggled to stay alive, the greatest search in Canadian Aviation history was launched. The manpower called upon to save the lives of the eight men was astounding.

MacAlpine witnessed the resourcefulness of those around him, and his vision of what would make Canada into a great nation changed. The resources that he discovered were not precious metals but a disparate group of men and women — the Inuit, the RCMP, the Dominion Explorers, the Hudson's Bay Company, Northern Aerial Mineral Exploration, Consolidated Mining and Smelting, and Western Canada Airways — all of whom had joined forces to achieve the common goal of the safe return of the eight men from the clutches of the vast Arctic wilderness.

The Arctic, to most, is a place that exists only as an idea in the imagination or on a map. For many, it is an image of snowy nothingness, rather than a physical location at the top of the world. But to the bush pilots and prospectors of the 1920s and 30s, the Arctic was filled with tremendous potential, and through their fortitude and foresight, they helped to develop the mineral assets that MacAlpine had sought. These individuals lived the idea.

The search and rescue of 1929 set a record, still unbroken, for the miles flown and number of planes and pilots involved in a search and rescue mission.[12] It also holds the title of the greatest aerial search in Canadian history and set an unbroken record for cost. Thayer Lindsley personally paid over half of the $400,000 price tag of the rescue.[13] This amount in today's dollars, using the price of gold as the standard, would be in excess of twenty-one million dollars.

The impressive understanding of flying in winter conditions that was gathered during the search from the Dominion Explorers was worth the cost. It would serve as a benchmark for not only the world to use as the airplane became pivotal both in exploration and in daily transportation, but also for future prospecting in Canada. For the next several years, Canadian pilots would be the leaders in aerial transportation, prospecting, and their vast experience would be drawn upon as aviation developed in North America and around the world.

Almost immediately after the start of the Depression, mining became a central economic driver in Canada, affecting development, research, culture, the environment, and peoples' livelihoods, not just in the North, but throughout the country. It still is.[14]

This expedition was the spark that ignited the interest of a nation and which highlighted the inventiveness, courage, humility, and compassion of its people's character. It is these traits that have made Canada a country that, though young, has carved a unique identity in the world.

| Epilogue |

Andy Cruickshank was sitting in his Prince George office, writing his "Pilot's Instructions" for passenger flights. Since he was training a new generation of pilots, he was developing a manual to assist in their classroom study. The topic he was working on was "Takeoff."

1. Taxi slowly. Passengers are given unpleasant sensations if planes are taxied faster than 10 miles per hour over rough fields.
2. Use all available area for take-off. When plane is in position for take-off it should be stopped and the brakes set and the motor run at full throttle, testing both magnetos. This is a precaution which is required by the Department of Commerce on all air lines in the United States, and passengers

riding lines regularly are aware of the significance of this procedure and expect it. As we are carrying through passengers from the States, it is necessary that we conform, apart from this it is good practice.

Cruickshank continued to list the important details that a pilot should be aware of and follow. He wrote that passengers may become frightened if the pilot turns the plane too close to the ground, and that any banks should be made at an angle no greater than 30 degrees. Holding the plane steady would help in reducing the possibility of air sickness, as would keeping the aircraft at an altitude that avoids bumpy air. Cruickshank's final point was that the pilot must take an interest in the passengers' well-being, and a good way to do that is to inform them of the distance travelled, and any interesting points in the landscape below. It was his belief that pilots should indicate a willingness to answer questions that any passenger asks of him, adding that this, too, adds to the pleasure of the flight.

Once he was satisfied with the instructions, he stacked his notes and picked up the package that sat on his desk. It had come from Dominion Explorers in Toronto on a WCA flight and was addressed to Captain and Mrs. Andrew Cruickshank. The parcel was wrapped in brown paper and was bulky and intriguing, but Cruickshank wanted to wait until he was at home with Esmé before he opened it.

He tidied up his desk, said goodbye to the employees of WCA, and headed to his car. He looked forward to this part of the day, as he headed home to his family. The drive was short and before long he was pulling up alongside of his tiny dwelling. Home was welcoming and warm, and smelled of something savoury bubbling on the stovetop. The fire crackled and instantly Cruickshank felt the comforts of his surroundings. Hellos and hugs took some time, and then he and Esmé sat at the kitchen table to open the package together. In it was a letter from Thayer Lindsley, a little velvet pouch, and a square box. They opened the letter first and read what had been written.

Karram Family Collection.

Andy Cruickshank and a new generation of "student" pilots stand outside a house in Swanson Bay, located on the Inside Passage in British Columbia.

Lindsley expressed his great appreciation for Cruickshank's excellent service during the search for the MacAlpine party. He wrote about the hazardous conditions and observed that Cruickshank had indeed placed his own life in danger for the sake of others. He continued that he held Cruickshank in the "very highest esteem" and relayed that there was no really adequate recompense for his involvement, but that he would like to give Cruickshank five hundred shares of Ventures Limited as a "small reward" for his services. He also asked that this be kept as a private matter between the two of them, since he did not want any publicity surrounding the gift. This would prove to be a substantial offering.[1] The gift was a generous one, but the letter behind it held even more significance to Cruickshank. For him, respect from another was the highest form of tribute. Esmé would hold onto those shares for decades.

Next, Esmé opened the velvet pouch and out fell matching gold nugget earrings. The nuggets, each measuring roughly one inch, were hung simply from a gold post. These were from MacAlpine, and given with his thanks for the support she showed to her husband during the search. Cruickshank had been able to devote the time and energy to the job at hand, knowing his wife was in control of their family, and MacAlpine was aware of the sacrifice Esmé was willing to make as her husband flew into the Arctic. The earrings, worn by Esmé throughout her life, were passed down to her daughter Dawn and then on to granddaughter Kerry-Dawn, who wore them on her wedding day. They remain a cherished family keepsake.

Cruickshank opened his box and inside was a gold cigarette case. He held the case in his hands and ran his fingers over the initials ADC that had been engraved on the front of the case. Cruickshank recalled the nights he spent with MacAlpine at Burnside and at Fort Reliance. Smoking served a two-fold purpose in the North. In the summer the smoke helped to ward off mosquitoes and other pesky insects, and during the winter months smoking was a social pastime. Cruickshank carried this case with him for the remainder of his life — a reminder of the great adventure in which he had played a major role. The case now belongs to grandson Edward.

MacAlpine's thoughtfulness and appreciation extended over the years and he never forgot the men and women who worked tirelessly on his behalf. This was evident in an interview with Domex pilot Stanley MacMillan. MacMillan, years later, recalled the fortitude and "legend of Colonel MacAlpine's leadership … he was our tower of strength and quickly formulated the disciplines that would sustain us both physically and mentally." MacMillan continued that it was no easy adventure for MacAlpine and he suffered as much or more than most of the group, but "his leadership was unquestioned in act or in thought. It has often been said that even among the most enlightened peoples of this earth, the veneer of civilized behavior is thin. We didn't suffer any conspicuous peeling of this veneer but incidents did occur where one might say fractures developed. It was at such times that we found reason to be most grateful that Colonel MacAlpine was able to imbue us with the restraint necessary to keep our group intact."[2]

Decades later, an interesting study, funded by the National Science Foundation (2000), was undertaken and MacAlpine's leadership skills would once again be considered. The study was to assist with protocol for extended long-duration space missions. Concern about the sensitivity to psychosocial issues during confined space-life was mounting. By reviewing documented historical data, information was gathered to identify areas of possible conflict. Once areas were pinpointed, procedures would then be set in place to avoid deterioration and breakdown of human relations in the NASA space program. The diary of Richard Pearce, which detailed the assigned daily duties of each member, was used to examine the effects of the human interaction during the weeks that were spent confined in the extreme Polar environment. Major Baker and Colonel MacAlpine had assigned each man in the group a daily task to perform and essentially gave each one a purpose. In doing so, the group showed "No notable shifts in how the passage of time was experienced beyond some impatience expressed by some members of the party to cross newly forming ice to arrive at their intended destination."[3]

Since winter flying in the North was in its infancy, developing the rescue plan required thoughtful and careful discussion, yet it also needed a daring group of men that could implement each stage. There were no gas depots in the North, maps were primitive and inaccurate, and the magnetic pole rendered compass readings useless. Wireless communications were few and far between. Plane engines had not been experimented with at these latitudes and temperatures or for such a long duration. Change over from floats to skis without the equipment found in aerodrome hangers had not been attempted. It was all new and the lessons learned in the Arctic, a land long shrouded in mystery, would require brutal hard work, resourcefulness and simple determination. These men, both determined and self-reliant, changed the course of aviation history, and with it the course of Canada. Remarkable as it may seem, something as simple as having four more gallons of gas in the planes would have enabled the Dominion Explorer expedition planes to reach Cambridge Bay and the search and rescue would never have been called out, and the lessons never learned, possibly postponing the development of the vast rich mineral deposits that would become one of the main contributors to Canada's economy.

Three years following the Domex rescue, the bush-pilot community would be rocked by the sudden and tragic deaths of several aviation heroes.

On June 29, 1932, Andy Cruickshank left the mining camp at Great Bear Lake on a three-hour flight to Fort Rae. His plane was overloaded and his fuel was reduced to accommodate the load. The engine on G-CASL he was flying had been changed just two days prior to the flight, and although Cruickshank had reported to the engineers that there was something seriously wrong with the engine after he tested it, he was instructed by his boss to fly the aircraft. Cruickshank told Esmé he would not sign the log book as his formal acknowledgement that the plane was not airworthy. His gut feeling once again was correct.

He took off with two engineers, Harry King and Horace Torrie, into a clear sky. Just twenty minutes before his destination was reached his engine died. He never made Fort Rae. Just short of a tiny lake, in the Northwest Territories, Cruickshank's plane fell from the sky. The tangled wreckage showed he had been trying to bring his plane to a safe landing on a lake close to Lake Mazenod. All three were killed. They were the first fatalities for Western Canada Airways Ltd.

Cruickshank and Torrie's combined funeral was held in Edmonton in early July 1932 and was marked by military rites. Cruickshank's casket was draped with the British flag, representing his service in the war, and bore the cap and sword he had worn. His casket rested on a gun carriage, and behind the carriage was a horse draped in black with boots reversed in the stirrups as a mark of Cruickshank's service with the Royal Canadian Mounted Police. Members of the RCMP, clad in their ceremonial red serge, marched in the funeral procession with the 19th Alberta Dragoons. Edmonton's militia officers also marched in the procession to the muffled drumbeats and music of the 49th Battalion Edmonton regimental band. Six airplanes flew over the procession. Pilot Hollick-Kenyon then brought his plane down low, over the grave, in the funeral salute of the air. At the burial, the firing party fired three volleys, a bugler sounded the last post, and the military men then gave their final salutes.

A Department of National Defense enquiry showed that the engine that had been installed on 'SL was the old engine from 'SP, the aircraft that sank in Churchill Harbour during the Dominion Explorers Expedition. The court documents continually questioned the airworthiness of 'SP's engine after its immersion in salt water. However, the fact remained — the engine had been put back into service and installed on 'SL just two days prior to the Fort

Rae flight. The cause of Western Canada Airways first fatal crash remains unsolved. Esmé and her two young daughters, Dawn aged three, and June aged one, were left on their own.

Bill Spence, during a winter Arctic flight, crashed into the white nothingness. He and his air engineer were killed instantly. J.D. Vance and his engineer caught a wing during a routine lake landing, sending his plane cart wheeling into the watery depths. Bill Nadin, with pilot Calder, also succumbed to an untimely death in a tragic crash on the same Great Bear–Fort Rae run as Cruickshank and his crew.

Reverend Canon Comyn-Ching from St. John's Church, Fort McMurray, paid tribute to Andrew Cruickshank and Horace Torrie at their funeral, and his words would easily apply to all the men who devoted their lives to being a bush pilot:

> Greater still they belong to that noble company of pathfinders who blaze a trail through to the ends of the earth. This North Country will ever be indebted to the part they played in its future. No glorification of self, no note of boastfulness or blatancy, but a deep love of adventure and discovery doing just another days work. In building the north they did not expect to see the happy ending themselves, theirs was only the far off [Mount] Pisgah view of it, but you who are their kinsmen will think with pride that they were privileged to give their lives that through them it might remain an inheritance for the generations to come ... and yet up there amid the crash of stars, they did their work well, unwavering vision of the end to work for, with every quality of self-sacrifice and heroic resolve, going forth on their knightly quest of the north — following the Holy Grail of the great adventure.[4]

| Appendix |

The People Involved

A. Cruickshank's Search and Rescue Party

Western Canada Airways Ltd.:
Andy Cruickshank (pilot) and **Alf Walker** (mechanic) flying the G-CASQ ('SQ).
Roy Brown (pilot) and **Paul Davis** (mechanic) flying G-CASO ('SO).
"Bertie" Hollick-Kenyon (pilot) and **Bill Nadin** (mechanic) flying G-CASL ('SL).
Pat Semple (mechanic) accompanied Cruickshank when he joined the search at Stony Rapids.
Tommy Siers (head mechanic for Western Canada Airways).

Northern Aerial Mineral Exploration:
Jim Vance (pilot) and **B.C. Blasdale** (mechanic) flying G-CARK ('RK).

Dominion Explorers:
Guy Blanchet (surveyor), field worker for Dominion Explorers.
Bill Spence (pilot) and **Graham Longley** (mechanic) flying CF-ACZ ('CZ).

Secondary personnel who joined in the last week (December 4) because of planes out of commission:
Ken Dewar (pilot) and **R. Niven** (mechanic) flying CF-AAM ('AAM), owned by Consolidated Mining and Smelting.
Charles Sutton (pilot) flying CF-AAN ('AAN), owned by Dominion Explorers.

B. The MacAlpine Party

Dominion Explorers:
Colonel Cyril MacAlpine, president of Dominion Explorers, flew in G-CASP until it sank, then flew in G-CASK. Leader of the expedition.
Major Robert "Bob" F. Baker, base manager who joined group at Baker Lake, flew in G-CASK.
E.A. "Brodie" Boadway, pilot and mining engineer, flew in CF-AAO.
Stan "Mac" MacMillan (pilot) and **Alexander "Alex" Milne** (mechanic) flying CF-AAO ('AO).
Richard Pearce, editor of *The Northern Miner*, observer and writer to record prospecting advances made by Dominion Explorers, kept a daily diary. Flew in 'SP then in 'SK.
Major G.A. "Tommy" Thompson (pilot) and **Don Goodwin** (mechanic) flew G-CASP then G-CASK.

C. Inuit "Saviours"

Awordiwo

Bunnuck

Helika

Kena

Keninya

Olga

Otoogo

Penukta

Tepinna

Tigalook

Tigatook

Unani

| NOTES |

Foreword

1. Eugenie Louise Myles, *Airborne from Edmonton* (Toronto: Ryerson Press, 1959), 144.

Chapter 1: Leaving for the Barrens

1. June Lunny, *Spirit of the Yukon* (Prince George, British Columbia: Caitlin Press, 1992), 60–61.

2. Guy Blanchet, *Search in the North* (Toronto: The Macmillan Company of Canada, 1960), 20.

3. Gwyneth Hoyle, *The Northern Horizons of Guy Blanchet: Intrepid Surveyor 1884–1966* (Toronto: Natural Heritage Books/Dundurn Press, 2007), 106.

4. *Ibid.*, 123.

5. Thayler Lindsley was born in 1882, in Yokohama, Japan.

When the family returned to the United States he attended Harvard University and received a civil engineering degree in 1924. Described as a geological genius, he is known as the greatest mine developer and finder of all time. When Lindsley flew over the Barrens he saw mineral wealth and set in motion the development of the Canadian mining industry. See *www. mininghalloffame.ca/inductees/j-l/thayer_lindsley*.

6. Guy Blanchet, *Search in the North* (Toronto: The MacMillan Company, 1960), 148.
7. Stanley MacMillan, "Recollections of a Dominion Explorers Pilot," University of Guelph Library, Archival & Special Collections, XM1MSA129, File 1, 16.
8. *Ibid.*
9. *Ibid.*, 17.
10. Inuit Traditions & History, *www.windows2universe.org/earth/ polar/inuit_culture.html*.
11. K.M. Molson, *Pioneering in Canadian Air Transport* (Altona, Manitoba: D.W. Friesen and Sons, Ltd., 1974), 40.

Chapter 2: Preparations for the Search
1. Andy Cruickshank's personal diary, *The MacAlpine Search*, 3.
2. *Canadian Press*, quoting the Rector of St. John's Church, Fort McMurray, July 1932.
3. Excerpt from a letter to Mrs. Andrew Cruickshank Sr., August 15, 1923, sent from "Depot Division" RCMP, Regina.
4. *The Bulletin*, Vol. 4, No.1 (1932), 24. Published by Canadian Airways Limited.
5. Lunny, *Spirit of the Yukon*, 87.
6. Frank Ellis, *Canada's Flying Heritage* (Toronto: University of Toronto Press, 1954), 259.

Chapter 3: Grounded by Weather
1. H.C. "Pat" Semple's Recollections, 2. His recollections, about five pages in length, located in an unsorted box at the Aviation

Museum in Winnipeg and made available by Pat Semple's daughter, Trudie Terpening, Semple Family Collection.

2. Cruickshank's personal diary, *The MacAlpine Search*, 3.
3. Richard Pearce, *Marooned in the Arctic: Diary of the Dominion Explorers' Expedition to the Arctic* (diary, 1931), 24.
4. *Ibid.*, 27.
5. *Ibid.*
6. *Ibid.*, 30.
7. Blanchet, *Search in the North*, 162.
8. *Ibid.*, 163.
9. *Ibid.*, 164.
10. Roy Brown, "The Origin & Growth of WCA as I have Seen It", MHS Transactions Series 3, Number 14, (1957–58), 9.
11. Pearce, *Marooned in the Arctic*, 33.
12. *Ibid.*, 34.
13. *Ibid.*
14. *Ibid.*, 35.
15. *Ibid.*
16. Révillon Frères, established in 1793, was a French fur and luxury goods company with stores in New York, Paris, and London. In 1903, with furs becoming high demand in the fashion industry, the brothers set up posts in northern Canada and the Arctic for fur trading with the Native people. Révillon Frères were direct competition with the Hudson's Bay Company. See GeoTourism Canada, *www.geotourismcanada. com*.
17. Molson, *Pioneering in Canadian Air Transport*, 80.
18. Gord Emberely, email message to author, December 6, 2010.
19. Andy Cruickshank's personal diary, *The MacAlpine Search*, 5.

Chapter 4: Moving Northward
1. Vilhjalmur Stefansson, *The Friendly Arctic* (Toronto: Macmillan Company of Canada, 1921).
2. Pearce, *Marooned in the Arctic*, 42.

3. *Ibid.*, 42–43.
4. Molson, *Pioneering in Canadian Air Transport*, 80.
5. *Ibid.*, 80.
6. H.C. "Pat" Semple, "Recollection," 2.
7. Countries and their Cultures, *www.everyculture.com/multi/Ha-La/Inuit.html.*
8. Blanchet, *Search in the North*, 73.
9. Pearce, *Marooned in the Arctic*, 44.
10. Blanchet, *Search in the North*, 75.
11. *Ibid.*, 76.
12. *Ibid.*, 114.

Chapter 5: Crash of G-CASQ
1. Blanchet, *Search in the North*, 126.
2. *Ibid.*, 166.
3. Philip H. Godsell, *Pilots of the Purple Twilight* (Calgary, Alberta: Fifth House Ltd., A Fitzhenry & Whiteside Company, 2003), 140.
4. Pearce, *Marooned in the Arctic*, 47.

Chapter 6: Peril on Ice
1. Andy Cruickshank's personal diary, *The MacAlpine Search*, 8.
2. Molson, *Pioneering in Canadian Air Transport*, 81.
3. Archives of Manitoba, "Search in Connection with the Lost MacAlpine Party," Western Canada Airways Ltd., MG11, A321, Box 37.
4. Blanchet, *Search in the North*, 170.
5. Molson, *Pioneering in Canadian Air Transport*, 81.
6. Lunny, *Spirit of the Yukon*, 119.
7. *Ibid.*
8. Molson, *Pioneering in Canadian Air Transport*, 81.
9. *Ibid.*
10. Semple, "Recollections," 7.
11. Lunny, *Spirit of the Yukon*, 119.

12. "One of the boys is in bad shape. His arm is numb, and his finger and eye muscles contracted. The Colonel felt that strain was at the bottom of the attack and that the boy was at the breaking point. He was given strong emergency dope. The Colonel slipped out to the other igloo several times, to see how the patient was breathing in his sleep...." Richard Pearce, *Marooned in the Arctic*, 49.

Chapter 7: Arrival at Cambridge Bay

1. "Marooned in the Arctic," *The CAHS Journal*, Vol. 15, No. 3 (1977), 83. Published by the Canadian Aviation Historical Society.
2. Blanchet, *Search in the North*, 171–72.
3. Tom Avery, *To the End of the Earth* (New York: St. Martin's Press, 2009), 111.
4. *Ibid.*
5. *Ibid.*, 259.
6. Frederick B. Watt, *Great Bear: A Journey Remembered* (Yellowknife, Northwest Territories: Outcrop Ltd., 1980), 85.
7. Frank Ellis, *Canada's Flying Heritage* (Toronto: University of Toronto Press, 1954), 257.
8. Canalaska was a trading company in direct competition with the Hudson's Bay Company. As part of their business, they loaned traps to the Inuit.
9. Godsell, *Pilots of the Purple Twilight*, 93.
10. Blanchet, *Search in the North*, 172.
11. Andy Cruickshank's personal diary, *The MacAlpine Search*, 11.
12. Ellis, *Canada's Flying Heritage*, 261.
13. Blanchet, *Search in the North*, 172.

Chapter 8: Evacuation Planning

1. Blanchet, *Search in the North*, 175.
2. Pearce, *Marooned in the Arctic*, 55.
3. *Ibid.*, 56.

4. Blanchet, *Search in the North*, 174.
5. "The MacAlpine Search Concluded," *The CAHS Journal*, Vol. 15, No. 3 (1977), 86.
6. *Ibid.*
7. Pearce, *Marooned in the Arctic*, 57.
8. Molson, *Pioneering in Canadian Transport*, 78.
9. Andy Cruickshank's personal diary, *The MacAlpine Search*, 12.

Chapter 9: Airborne to Fort Reliance
1. Andy Cruickshank's personal diary, *The MacAlpine Search*, 14.
2. Richard Pearce, "Marooned in the Arctic: A Northern Rescue," *Altitude*, Vol. 33, No. 1 (2007), 10. Published by Western Canada Aviation Museum.
3. *Man Vs. Wild, Iceland*, Season 1, Episode 11, Discovery Channel. (November 2010). Television series about men surviving in extreme climates.
4. Semple, "Recollections," 9.
5. "Marooned in the Arctic: A Northern Rescue," *Altitude*, 10.
6. Blanchet, *Search in the North*, 180.
7. Pearce, *Marooned in the Arctic*, 63.
8. Sir George Back (1796–1878) was a British naval officer, Arctic explorer, and artist. He was selected by John Franklin for the overland Arctic Expedition of 1819. After this experience, Back continued to explore the frozen lands of Canada's North, surveying the Arctic Ocean coastline. During one of the later trips he set up a wintering station at the eastern end of Great Slave Lake called Fort Reliance. The Back River was named for him. The new Fort Reliance, established in the general vicinity of a Back's 1833 fort, was a community with a RCMP station, some fur traders and buildings that were part of the Domex base. See Dictionary of Canadian Biography Online.
9. Andy Cruickshank's personal diary, *The MacAlpine Search*, 15.
10. *Ibid.*, 16.
11. Blanchet, *Search in the North*, 181.

12. *Ibid.*
13. Semple, "Recollections," 9.
14. Blanchet, *Search in the North*, 192.
15. "Marooned in the Arctic: A Northern Rescue," *Altitude*, 10.
16. Blanchet, *Search in the North*, 183.
17. *Ibid.*
18. *Ibid.*, 184.
19. *Ibid.*, 185.

Chapter 10: Two More Planes Down
1. Blanchet, *Search in the North*, 190.
2. Andy Cruickshank's personal diary, *The MacAlpine Search*, 20.
3. *Ibid.*, 21.
4. Blanchet, *Search in the North*, 185.
5. *Ibid.*, 186.
6. *Ibid.*, 187.
7. *Ibid.*
8. *Ibid.*, 186.
9. *Ibid.*, 189.
10. Andy Cruickshank's personal diary, *The MacAlpine Search*, 23.
11. Pearce, "Marooned in the Arctic: A Northern Rescue," *Altitude*, 10.
12. *Ibid.*, 11.
13. Blanchet, *Search in the North*, 191.
14. *Ibid.*
15. *Ibid.*
16. Andy Cruickshank's personal diary, *The MacAlpine Search*, 24.

Chapter 11: A Crowded Journey Home
1. Pearce, *Marooned in the Arctic*, 68.
2. Andy Cruickshank's personal diary, *The MacAlpine Search*, 24.
3. Blanchet, *Search in the North*, 194.
4. The modern-day Iditarod race runs between Anchorage, in south-central Alaska, and Nome, Alaska, on the western

Bering Sea. It has been called "The Last Great Race" and takes the musher between ten and seventeen days to complete the 1,150-kilometre distance. The dogs and their musher cross mountain ranges, frozen rivers, through dense forests, and across the desolate tundra. The trail the teams travel was the one used by miners in the 1920s. See the Official Site of the Iditarod: *www.iditarod.com.*

5. Excerpt written by Andy Cruickshank to his mother, Mrs. (Emily) Andrew Cruickshank, Sr., Y Division Yukon Territory, dated March 30, 1926. Karram family Collection.

6. "First of Arctic Explorers' Party on Way Home — Hard Luck on Way Out," *The Northern Miner*, December 5, 1929, 1.

7. Blanchet, *Search in the North*, 194.

8. "Second Contingent of MacAlpine Party Will Reach Winnipeg Today," *The Manitoba Free Press*, December 5, 1929, 1.

9. "Rescue and Search Pilots Reach City," *The Manitoba Free Press*, December 6, 1929, 6.

10. "Relatives of Missing Explorers Overjoyed," *The Manitoba Free Press*, November 5, 1929, 11.

11. "Real Romance at Re-union of Gallant Explorers and Their Brave Women Folk," *The Manitoba Free Press*, December 7, 1929, 10.

12. Hoyle, *The Northern Horizons of Guy Blanchet*, 138.

13. George Norrie and Harry Norrie, *From Cloddy Earth to Glittering Gold* (Saint John, New Brunswick: Trinity Enterprise Inc., 2006), 214.

14. Government of Canada. Mining in Canada: *www.canadainternational.gc.ca/guatemala/commerce_canada/mining-exploitation_miniere.aspx?lang=eng.*

Epilogue

1. In 1928, Thayer Lindsley paid 2.5 million dollars for mining claims for Ventures Limited. Ventures Limited incorporated Falconbridge into its holdings that same year, with Thayer Lindsley as president and director. In 1962, Ventures Limited

merged with Falconbridge and became one of the largest mining companies in the world. The stock shares reflected the value of this giant mining company. Lindsley served as president and a director until 1967, when he accepted the position of director emeritus. See Canadian Mining Hall of Fame, *www.mininghalloffame.ca.*

2. Archival & Special Collections University of Guelph Library, Stanley MacMillan Recollections of a Dominion Explorers Pilot, XM1MS A129, File 1, 19.

3. Ten Missions, Two Studies Crew Composition, Time, and Subjective Experience in Mars-Analog Expeditions: *www.pweb.jps.net/~gangale/opsa/TenMissionsTwoStudies/TenMissionsTwoStudiesFrm.htm.*

4. Reverend Canon Comyn-Ching of St. John's Church, Fort McMurray, eulogy notes from Cruickhank/Torrie Funeral, July 1929. Karram Family Collection. "Pisgah" is a reference to the Old Testament, Deuteronomy 3:21–24, the Lord instructs Moses to go to the top of Mount Pisgah.

| Bibliography |

1. Articles, Papers, Reports

Archival & Special Collections, University of Guelph Library, Stanley MacMillan Recollections of a Dominion Explorers Pilot, XM1MS A129, File 1, 19.

Archives of Manitoba, "Search in Connection with the Lost MacAlpine Party." Western Canada Airways Ltd., MG11, A321, Box 37.

Brown, Roy. "The Origin & Growth of WCA as I have Seen It." *MHS Transactions* Series 3, Number 14, (1957–58), 9.

The Bulletin. Vol. 4, No.1 (1932): 24. Tribute to the three men who died in the crash of 'SL. Published by Canadian Airways Limited.

Gibson, Ginger and Jason Klinck. "Canada's Resilient North: The Impact of Mining on Aboriginal Communities." *Pimatisiwin: A Journal of Aboriginal and IndigenousCommunity Health*, Vol. 3, No. 1 (Spring 2005). *www.pimatisiwin.com/online/?page_id=444.*

Man Vs. Wild. "Episode 11: Iceland," Discovery Channel. November 2010.

"Marooned in the Arctic." *The CAHS Journal.* Vol. 15, No. 3 (1977). Published by the Canadian Aviation Historical Society.

Pearce, Richard, "Marooned in the Arctic: A Northern Rescue." *Altitude,* Vol. 3, No. 1 (2007).

Spence, Bill. "Recollections." *Altitude,* Vol. 33, No.1 (2007): 10–11.

Western Canada Archives, "The MacAlpine Search Concluded." *The CAHS Journal,* Vol. 15, No. 3, (1977).

2. Books

Avery, Tom. *To The End of the Earth.* New York: St. Martin's Press, 2009.

Blanchet, Guy. *Search in the North.* Toronto: The Macmillan Company, 1960.

Ellis, Frank. *Canada's Flying Heritage.* Toronto: University of Toronto Press, 1954.

Godsell, Philip H. *Pilots of the Purple Twilight.* Calgary: Fifth House Ltd., A Fitzhenry & Whiteside Company, 2003.

Hoyle, Gwyneth. *The Northern Horizons of Guy Blanchet: Intrepid Surveyor 1884–1966.* Toronto: Natural Heritage Books/ Dundurn Press, 2007.

Lunny, June. *Spirit of the Yukon.* Prince George, British Columbia: Caitlin Press, 1992.

Molson, K.M. *Pioneering in Canadian Air Transport.* Altona, Manitoba: D.W. Friesen and Sons, Ltd., 1974.

Norrie, George and Harry Norrie. *From Cloddy Earth to Glittering Gold.* Saint John, New Brunswick: Trinity Enterprise Inc., 2006.

Pearce, Richard. *Marooned in the Arctic: Diary of the Dominion Explorers' Expedition to the Arctic.* Toronto: self-published, 1931.

Stefannson, Vilhjalmur. *The Friendly Arctic.* Toronto: Macmillan Company of Canada, 1921.

Watt, Frederick B. *Great Bear: A Journey Remembered.* Yellowknife, Northwest Territories: Outcrop Ltd., 1980.

3. Newspapers

The Manitoba Free Press.

"Eight Planes to Make Systematic Hunt for Men Missing in North." September 23, 1929.

"History Surrounds Northern Post Where Explorers Where Found." November 5, 1929.

"Intrepid Airmen Plan Desperate Attack On Secrets Of Far North." October 2, 1929.

"News of Safety of MacAlpine Party." November 22, 1929.

"Real Romance at Re-union of Gallant Explorers and Their Brave Women Folk." December 7, 1929.

"Second Contingent of MacAlpine Party Will Reach Winnipeg Today." December 6 1929.

"Work of Organizing Hunt for Lost Fliers Advances." September 25,1929.

The Northern Miner.

"Arctic Party Battles Its Own Hungry Way to Safety." November 7,1929.

"Confident Arctic Party Safe Though Down; Relief Ships Out." September 26 1929, 1.

"First of Arctic Explorers' Party on Way Home — Hard Luck on Way Out", December 5, 1929, 1.

"To the Flying Sourdoughs." January 23, 1930, 18.

"Winter Grips North and Stays Hands of Rescuers." October 10, 1929, 1.

4. Websites

Countries and their Cultures, *www.everyculture.com/multi/Ha-La/Inuit.htmal.*

GeoTourism Canada, Inuit Traditions & History, *www.geotourismcanada.com.*

Indian Traditions and their Cultures. *www.windows2universe.org/earth/polar/inuit_culture.html.*

Mining Hall of Fame, *www.mininghalloffame.ca/inductees/j-lthayer_lindsley*.

Bishop, Sheryl, Marilyn Dudley-Rowley, Kristin Farry, Thomas Gangale, and Patrick Nolan. "Ten Missions, Two Studies Crew Composition, Time, and Subjective Experience in Mars-Analog Expeditions." University of South Carolina, The University of Texas Medical Branch, *www.ops-alaska.com/TenMissionsTwoStudiesFrm.htm*.

Jones, J Sydney, "Inuit," Countries and Their Cultures, *http://www.everyculture.com/multi/Ha-La/Inuit.html*.

| INDEX |

About the Author

Kerry Karram with her dog Becker.

Kerry Karram is the fourth generation of her family to live at the foot of Grouse Mountain in North Vancouver, British Columbia. Growing up, walking the trails and seeing the wild life instilled in her a love for nature. She lives in the family home with her husband Michael and children. Her four dogs help to make a full house.

Kerry has done public relations for a large company, and during her leisure time continues to teach handwork, design patterns, and publish quilting articles.

Writing a book was something that, as a child, Kerry had told her grandmother she would do one day. In 2008, she discovered her grandfather Andy Cruickshank's diary tucked inside a worn, yellowed envelope. Fascinated, she put her graduate studies on hold and, using the diary as one of her sources, began to write *Four Degrees Celsius*. Her deep interest in Canadian history and her love for the Far North is reflected in her writing.

She is currently working on her second book.

Of Related Interest

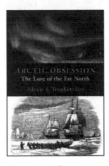

Arctic Obsession
The Lure of the Far North
by Alexis S. Troubetzkoy
9781554888559
$35.00

More than an account of the human delusion and fortitude in penetrating one of the most inhospitable areas of the world, *Arctic Obsession* goes beyond the gripping history of northern exploration, of the searches for the Northwest and Northeast Passages. From early medieval times to the twenty-first century, what has been the beguiling attraction of the North? What manner of men were they who boldly ventured into those hostile and unpredictable regions, scores never to return home, swallowed up by the merciless north. Today's Arctic is developing into tomorrow's hot spot. *Arctic Obsession* dwells on contemporary issues besetting the most fragile part of our globe — global warming and environmental, ecological and geo-political concerns. The book also provides an overview of the entire Arctic region, from Canada, Russia, and Alaska to Greenland, Iceland, and the North Sea.

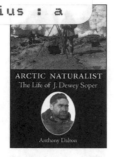

Arctic Naturalist
The Life of J. Dewey Soper
by Anthony Dalton
9781554887460
$29.99

Dewey Soper first travelled to the Arctic in 1923. During the next seven years he accepted three research postings on Baffin Island, each of which lasted between one and two years. In 1929 he discovered the breeding grounds of the blue goose in the southwest corner of Baffin Island. He also charted the final unknown region of Baffin Island's coastline. Later in life he worked in the western Arctic. Outside the Far North, Soper studied bison in Wood Buffalo National Park, documented bird life on the Prairies, and made a detailed study of small mammals in Alberta.

Soper was the last of the great pioneer naturalists in Canada. He was also a skilled and meticulous explorer. As a naturalist, he was a major contributor to the National Museum of Canada, as well as to the University of Alberta and other museums across the country.

Available at your favourite bookseller.

DUNDURN
www.dundurn.com

What did you think of this book?
Visit www.dundurn.com for reviews, videos, updates, and more!